definitive
guide to the
internet

FKB Publishing
F2 Wellpark, Willeys Avenue, Exeter, EX2 8BE

© **2000 FKB Publishing Ltd.**

Author: Paul Bartlett
Editor: Johnny Morrisey
Sub Editor: Ina Oltack
Graphics: Mark James
Contributors: Jade Edwards, Andrew Dixon, Greg Moxham, Paul Crabtree and
Julie Porter

ISBN 1 902160 25 8

Printed and bound in the UK by The Bath Press.

definitive
guide to the
internet

the definitive guide to surfing the internet for PC and Mac

Contents

1-Internet Basics

The History of the Internet 6
What's online then? 8
Who owns the Internet? 10
What sort of privacy do I have? 10
The Main Internet Services 11
Internet Addresses and Domain Names . .12
Common concerns 14

2-Getting Connected

What is needed to connect? 17
How to get connected 19
The price of using the Internet 24
How to connect 25
ISDN 25
The Web Browser 26
Troubleshooting 27
What else will I need? 27

3-Surfing the Web

The make-up of a Web Page 29
Home Pages 32
Bookmarks/Favourites 32
The Status Bar 32
How to use a Web Browser 33
A little about Web Addresses 34
Links and Buttons 35
History Files and the Cache 35
Image Maps 36
Saving Files 36
404 - Not found! 37
Search Engines & Directories 37
Personalising 39
Multiple Search Engines 40
Buying online 40
Buying Smart 42
Auctions .42
Using the Web to Download Software . . .35
Buying from Abroad 44

Earning money online 44
Plugins 46
Java 47
Cookies 48
Browser settings 48
True interaction on the World Wide Web .49
Censorship 49
Web-Based Email 50
Off-line Browsing 50
Anonymity 50
Virus worries 51

4-Email

What is email? 52
What will you need? 52
Setting up 53
Sending files 55
Freemail 57
Organising your email 59
General tips 59
Dealing with Spam 60
Video & Audio 62
Mailing Lists 63
Virus hoaxes 64
Anonymous Remailers 65
A recap of email netiquette 65

5-Newsgroups

What you will need 68
The Software 68
Subscribing 70
The Groups 70
Do I have access to every group? 71
Threads 71
Files 72
Netiquette 72
DejaNews .74
How to avoid getting spam 74
Reading offline 75

Kill Files 75

6-Downloading Software
What is FTP? 77
How do I use it? 77
What's this about being anonymous? . . .78
Uploading your web site 78
Text connections 78
Binary or Ascii? 81
Downloading via the Web 81
WinZip 82

7-Chat
What is it all about? 83
IRC 84
The Networks 85
The Channels 85
The Software 85
Setting Up 85
DCC 87
Talkers 88
So what's Telnet? 88
The first steps 88
Web Chat .91
ICQ 93

8-Online Gaming
Quake III - Tips 95
Unreal Tournement- Tips 96
Tribes 97
Half-Life - Tips 97
Wireplay .98
How do I connect to Wireplay? 99
Using Wireplay 99
EidosNet .101

9-MP3
What do I need to play Mp3s? 102
Why all the excitement about Mp3? . . .102

Finding Mp3s 103
Making Mp3s 104
WinAmp Extentions 104
Listening over the Internet 105

10-Movies on your PC
Playing movies on your PC 106

11-Game Emulators
What you need 108
Machines that can be emulated 109
Arcade Games 110
Computers 110
Early Consoles 111
Modern Systems 112
N64/UltraHLE 112
PSX/Bleem 113
Resources .113

12-Your Own Web Site
Where to put it 114
How to Write it 115
HTML 116
The easy way 120
Design tips 121
General tips 122

13-Promoting Business Online
Walking the tightrope 123
Setting Up 123
Designing a site 124
Promoting your site 126

Web Site Directory
Index 128

Glossary

Abbreviations & Smileys

1-Internet Basics

The original Definitive Guide to the Internet was published in 1999. The information has had to be completely updated for this 2000 version. This is testament to how quickly the whole online world is expanding. In the past twelve months we've seen a revolution in the way we access the Internet, and things are only going to get better. No longer do we have to pay phone bills to access the Internet, and the ultra-fast ADSL connections are just around the corner. Still, let's not get ahead of ourselves.

The History of the Internet

The Internet started out in the sixties. Original development began in the UK, but it was soon moved to the US for funding purposes. It was created so that military computers could be linked up effectively, with little risk of network failure. Old style networks were like a chain, in that they were only as strong as the weakest link. The problem was that if nuclear attack or whatever else destroyed one of the computers in the chain, the whole network would cease to function. As a remedy to this potentially dangerous situation, the computer bods devised something called TCP, which sends data from one machine to another via the quickest route. So, if one computer in the chain is taken out, it'll simply find another way around.

Later, it was opened up to universities. Initially this was only throughout America, but soon the Internet began to spread around the world. The Web was still a very long way from being developed, and everything was strictly text-only. However, even then the potential of e-mail and global realtime communication was appreciated - if only by the nerds.

Tim Berners-Lee created the World Wide Web (or WWW, or just Web) in 1989. At first it was a simple affair, and very few people could access it - and even fewer would want to. The only Websites that existed were based around high-level physics and projects related to the CERN Institute where Berners-Lee worked. It had been developed so that the scientific community could share information in a more user-friendly way. It wasn't until a little while later that CERN put their World Wide Web technology into the Public Domain, allowing everybody to use it freely.

The Web was only opened up to the Internet community at large in 1993, and even then it remained unused by the vast majority until 1994, when Mosaic was released. Mosaic was a breakthrough in browser design, it was portable and easy to use, and the public immediately took to it. Naturally, it was in Mosaic's favour that it was the first major browser to be made available for Windows based PCs. The multimedia revolution had begun. The original browser was called WorldWideWeb, but this was changed to Nexus to avoid confusion between the technology and the Web browser. Things evolved gradually until the team that developed Mosaic went on to create Netscape, one of the most important Internet applications ever.

THE INTERNET WORLD INTERVIEW

Tim Berners-Lee

An unsentimental look at the medium he helped propel

By James C. Luh

At the dawn of a new century, the most romantic notions about the Internet business can only take a greater hold. Rules seem less certain, possibilities seem wider, and it seems less likely that anyone can predict today what the future holds.

If you want the best possible guess, though, you could do worse than ask Tim Berners-Lee, the man who created the foundation for the World Wide Web.

Internet World caught up with Berners-Lee in a midtown Manhattan diner while he was out promoting his recent book, "Weaving the Web," which recounts how today's Web grew out of technologies the London-born, Oxford-educated researcher designed in the early '90s at Switzerland's **European Laboratory for Particle Physics** (CERN).

The 20th century's answer to Gutenberg was unassuming, energetic, and jovial, taking advantage of a pause in our interview to snap a few photos of the scene with a digital camera, stretching out his arm and turning the camera around to get himself in the picture. The 44-year-old pioneer isn't just spending his time basking in the glory of the Web's first decade, though. In his role as director of the **World Wide Web Consortium** (W3C), he's also working assiduously for the future of his invention in the next decade and beyond.

Lately Berners-Lee has found himself talking frequently about his vision for the next phase of the Web's evolution, what he calls "the semantic Web." The bits and bytes of the semantic Web contain more than just raw content. In the semantic Web, meaning itself is embedded in the framework of the Web, and its infrastructure reflects and communicates the relationships among Internet resources. The W3C is working hard to create and promote base technologies for enabling the semantic Web, including XML and the Resource Description Framework (RDF), a "metadata" framework that allows semantic relationships to be expressed in structures that can be read and processed by computer programs.

Exactly what form Berners-Lee's semantic Web might take is still hard to pin down, but it has the potential to radically change the way people and machines interact with the Net and with

At around 1994, the older parts of the Internet started to die off. Telnet (a text-based way of communicating with other computers) and Archie (a file-searching tool) were two of the first casualties. These old fashioned ways of using the Internet were quickly superseded, with Telnet usage now being limited to tech-heads or chat fanatics (see the chapter on chat, starting at page 83). Archie was pretty much dead as early as 1996. The Web crushed everything in it's path, including the mighty File Transfer Protocol. Although FTP is often used today as a means of transferring files, the Web is responsible for infinitely more Internet 'traffic'.

Gradually, more and more companies started to sit up and take notice of the Internet and the possibilities for business that it presented. Some unscrupulous individuals resorted to mass emailing, but an ever increasing amount of reputable companies started to establish their companies online. These days, you'd be hard pushed to find a large company that doesn't have some sort of Web presence. Certainly, many of them are useless show pieces, and some look terrible, but these are still very early days.

What's online then?

Thankfully, it's not all commercial. A huge proportion of Web content is non-profit making, and it exists purely for the entertainment and education of others. Running a Website can be very rewarding, and if you do it well, it can even lead to decent (not to mention well paid) employment. For many though, it's the quest for fame and recognition that drives them on to create Websites. Be it a fan site for The Simpsons or a help forum for people with a particular illness, there's always someone willing to do the hard work.

The Web is only one side of the Internet, however. You can also play games online, and there are many people who believe that multi-player Quake/Half-Life/Unreal games played over the Internet provide the most entertainment for your money. Mindless killing is fun, naturally, but there's a lot more to the Internet than wholesale slaughter. No, really.

Chatting with people worldwide is also a very popular hobby. There are millions of people who log on to talk to people all around the globe - and it's great to be able to learn more about a foreign country through somebody who actually lives there! The Internet is a great place to make friends, especially since nobody has any pre-conceptions about you if they can't actually see you. There is a downside to this of course. That girl you've been talking to for six months, who claims to be a Cameron Diaz lookalike, could turn out to be a 20 stone male biker with hairy palms. However, if you stick to the reputable places, you should be fine.

No doubt you will have heard of couples having met originally on the Internet. Maybe you'll have seen 'You got Mail', with Tom Hanks and Meg Ryan. Well, it's not just a fairytale - these things happen all the time. Marriages between people who met online are happening so often that it's hardly even given a second thought by many people. True, it usually happens in the States, but it quite often happens in the UK too. Most people tend to keep it to themselves when they've met on the Internet, so we don't get to hear about most instances.

If you don't think you'd be up for marriage, it's easy enough to make new friends online, as you can see in the chapter about talkers and chat rooms on page 72. You could make friends with someone who lives in your street, or somebody who lives half way around the world. This is particularly useful for people who are shy, or due to illness, can't get out much. If you're the shy type, you'll no doubt find that the Internet makes finding friends a million times easier. You can really make life-long friends online, if you want to.

Students can find the Internet incredibly useful too. All universities and a lot of colleges offer free access, which should not be ignored. Even if you hate the idea of the Internet, you simply cannot afford to ignore its potential. Whatever you're studying, there are thousands of sources of information that can help you. It can speed up work tenfold, and there's no more boring copying of sources from books; you can copy from the browser and paste it into your work. There are even online language translators. They're hardly foolproof, but they could help you out of a fix.

It's not just the further-education gang that can benefit, either. Any parent who wants his or her children to do well in high school should invest in a computer and Internet connection. An added bonus is that children would most likely not complain about being given a new computer - but try unloading a batch of encyclopedias onto them, and see how far that gets you. If you don't believe that the Internet is a brilliant teaching tool, then try it for yourself. Go to AltaVista (http://www.altavista.com) and search for the subject of your choice - ie, "quantum physics" or "classical history". You're bound to be impressed.

If you're thinking of going on holiday, then you can use the Net to research your destination. You can make sure that it's safe, first of all. Then you can check out what other people think of your chosen area, and pick up some hints on where to go and what to do. Maybe ask around in travel Newsgroups. Some people will be sure to give you some advice. Then there's online booking. Flights and hotels can be checked for availability from the comfort of your own home, and prices are usually cheaper online.

All in all, the Internet is easily one of the best and cheapest forms of entertainment that you'll ever see. From playing games to getting the latest gossip, there are no limits to what the Internet has to offer. You can do your shopping without leaving the house, email your friends and colleagues, get the latest news before it appears on TV, download the latest video reports from CNN, and listen to your favourite UK radio station.

It really is that simple. There's no big deal. The Internet is staggeringly easy to use. Even someone with the most limited computer skills can use the Internet effectively - the only barrier is simple technophobia.

This book assumes that the reader has some small degree of knowledge when it comes to using their chosen computer; how to use the basic parts of the operating system for example. Don't be afraid to try things. Most people call ISP technical support because they're frightened of computers. They're afraid that by clicking the wrong button, they could wreck their machine. The key is to be a bit bolder. A computer is only as intelligent as the person using it. You need only be wary about the following things: deleting, uninstalling, and formatting. Since none of these things are relevant to this book, you have little to be concerned about.

It's easy to get confused about the Internet if you've never used it before. The truth is, the online world is infinitely simpler than the real life one. You can view the Web as a big magazine, where you click buttons to reach different pages, it's that simple.

Who owns the Internet?

The Internet has no regulating body. It's entirely run by the people that use it. The companies that offer access to the Internet don't run it, and there is no single person or body that can in any way affect its content. Not even the US Government, who have tried several times before.

Contrary to popular belief, AOL does not own the Internet, didn't establish the Internet, and doesn't regulate the Internet. In fact, aside from providing access to it (along with thousands of other companies) via their own front end, they have nothing to do with it.

What sort of privacy do I have?

Privacy on the Internet is more than adequate, but far from complete. Anyone who wanted to trace you having only information gained from your Internet connection would have a very difficult job, but it's not impossible. Bodies such as the police also have an easier time tracking people, but that's another matter entirely. It's not as though your name is splashed all over the place when you connect. You actually have a reasonably good layer of external protection. You don't need to tell anyone your name, you can keep your exact location to yourself too. It's quite possible for someone to find your country of origin, but that is no huge breach of privacy. Basically, you shouldn't really worry about it too much. Just be careful about where you put your real name and address. It's not difficult, just a case of using common sense. Never give out your full name, telephone number or address to anyone unless you trust them. In real life, you wouldn't go around giving your name and address to any Tom, Dick or Harry you come across, it's common sense. Try to use the same sense when online, but don't be paranoid.

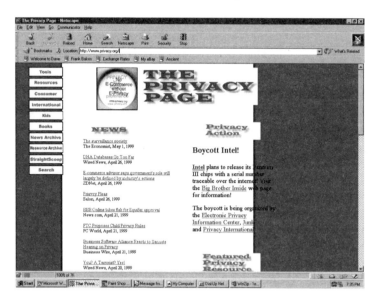

The Main Internet Services

The World Wide Web

The Web is the world's biggest source of information. Millions of pages of text, pictures, sounds and video. By using a piece of software called a Web Browser, you can easily navigate your way around, either for education or entertainment. Whether it's finding the latest gossip on your favourite soap or studying for an exam, the Web will be able to help you. To find out more about the Web, go to page 29.

Email

The quickest, most reliable, and cheapest form of communicating with people who aren't in the same room as yourself. Email has taken off to such an extent that it's fast taking over the role of the traditional postal service. Read more about email starting on page 52.

1 1

Newsgroups

Whatever your interest, there is probably a Newsgroup where like-minded people can discuss it. Working in a similar way to Email, Newsgroups are one of the best ways of communicating with large numberss of people. More is on page 67.

FTP

Now slightly outdated in many respects, FTP is the traditional method of transferring files (such as software) over the Internet. You can access FTP sites using all good Web browsers, or a dedicated piece of software. Read more on page 76.

Chat

Chatting with people in real time over the Internet is a very useful tool. You can discuss things with business associates, all of whom may be in different parts of the world, without delay. Chat is also good for making friends all around the world. It's much simpler than sending loads of emails, and an awful lot quicker. To read about chat, go to the more detailed explanation on page 83.

Online Gaming

Many people will have played Quake or Half Life, but these games come into their own when played over the Internet. You can slaughter your friends, relatives, or even total strangers. Just be careful with the phone bill! The online gameplaying begins on page 95.

Internet Addresses and Domain Names

This section may be a little confusing or difficult to understand - if you find that it's all a bit too much, don't worry - This is only being mentioned for completeness, and you don't need to have a 100% solid understanding of it to use the Internet.

Every machine on the Internet has it's own address. By this, we don't mean it's physical address. Every machine has to have it's own identity, so that other computers know how to communicate with it. It's best to imagine it like a postal address. When you send a letter (or piece of data), it is sent to the address (or computer) to which it is addressed. If it had no address, it would get lost. It's the same with the Internet.

Usually, these addresses are made up of three parts. Let's take this example:

computer.server.com

Note that there are no capital letters in that address - they are never needed. In this (fictitious) example address, 'server.com' is the domain name. People pay for their own domain names, which are a combination of one word (or series of words joined by dashes) followed by a three letter suffix. This suffix may be .com (company), .org (organisation), .gov (government) or .net (network). English sites often use .co.uk, and most other countries have their own suffixes. Once you have your own domain name, and a server to which it points (a machine that is permanently connected to the Internet), then you can also assign your own subdomains (in this case, 'computer'), without paying anything extra. 'Computer' would be another machine that is connected to the Internet, which needs a unique domain name of it's own.

Computers actually address other machines on the Internet with numbers, not words. They use something called a Domain Name Server to translate these words into numbers. Thankfully you need to know nothing about this in order to use the Internet.

If you want your own personal Domain Names these can be purchased from a variety of different companies. They can be bought from as little as £10 each, so shop around if you want one - but make sure you'll get good service. Use the Newsgroups (see page 67) to get some advice if you need it - but be warned, some of the people that try to advise you will probably be trying to sell you domains themselves! Sometimes, you get what you pay for. Make sure you check for hidden charges (such as the cost of transferring your domain name to another Web provider).

On the other hand, Some companies, such as FreeNetName (http://www.freenetname.co.uk) will give you a free domain name (and the Web space to use it with) for free, as long as you use their ISP services. The catch is that FreeNetName and the other free domain companies all charge nearly £100 to release your domain name to a different firm, and the Terms and Conditions go on forever! Read them carefully!

Finally, you should know how to say domain names. You do not say the domain name AltaVista.com as 'AltaVista-full-stop-com' or 'AltaVista com'. The correct way of saying it would be 'altavista dot com'. If you're talking about email addresses, then that's easy too. Bob@yahoo.com becomes 'Bob at Yahoo dot com'.

Common Concerns

No doubt you've heard plenty of scare mongering from various newspapers about the horrors of the Internet. In actual fact, unless you're of a severely nervous disposition, there's little to be scared of. However, you should always be a little careful. These are the main points of concern.

Pornography

There is pornography, and plenty of it. If pornography scares you, stay away from it. It's that simple. Nobody forces you to look at it. Most pornography sites contain very little in the form of uncensored hard-core action unless you have your credit card handy. Beware the dirty Newsgroups though. Whilst the majority are pretty tame (despite some of their names), there are a few that people will find upsetting. Parents may wish to restrict the access that children have to Intenet Relay Chat (IRC) (see page 84), as well.

The Virus Problem

Sad to say that many people in the world are bitter, lonely individuals that waste their lives trying to ruin things for everyone else. Some of these people, under the guise of being 'cool hackers' (even though they're generally ugly, slobbish teenagers) like to program Virii. A virus is a small computer program which attaches itself to another computer program and copies itself all over the place. It then does something nasty to the host computer. The damage could be instant, spread over a long period of time, or triggered on a certain date.

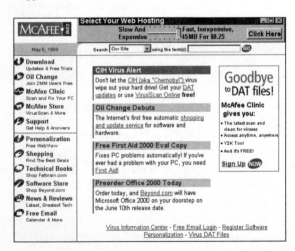

They are mainly transmitted through unsavoury channels; pirated software is a favourite way of distributing them. However, they can sometimes be contracted via other means. This is why it's best to install a decent piece of software, such as McAffee (available at http://www.mcaffee.com/), or Norton Antivirus (http://www.symantec.com/region/uk/). They're a pain in the backside, taking up system resources and always giving off false alarms - but they might just save the day. Almost everyone comes into contact with a virus at some point. Always, always check programs sent to you via email, and if they are sent to you by somebody you don't know, delete them immediately. It's not just viruses that you have to be afraid of, but Trojans. Named after the famous Trojan Horse legend of ancient Greece, Trojans give the appearance of being a normal program but when run they do something nasty to your computer. Don't be a victim. Don't run programs if you're not certain you trust the source. Even if you do trust the source, check it anyway.

There are some unpleasant virii doing the rounds at the moment. They transmit themselves by infecting your machine, and then emailing all of your friends and colleagues with a copy of the virus. These people, trusting you, may run the file sent to them, and then they become infected. And so it goes on. It cannot be stressed enough how important it is to get yourself a decent virus checker. It really is worth spending the money in order to get a good one. And, of course, when you've got one, you should always regularly update it. All good virus checkers provide regular updates from their Web sites, which ensure that you can always catch out the latest viruses before they do any damage. In case you were wondering, humans can't catch computer virii!

Security

If you have ever watched the X-Files or any of the glut of Hollywood efforts concerning hackers, you'd be forgiven for thinking that hacking into people's computers whilst connecting to the Internet is commonplace. In actual fact, it's more or less impossible. It becomes a problem if you're running a UNIX based operating system, but Windows users have very little to worry about. The worst anybody can realistically do is to crash your machine - and to do that they'd need to know your IP address (see the previous section on Domain Names and addresses). Besides, the only reason that somebody might do this is if they really didn't like you - it doesn't happen randomly. However, you should be wary of something called Back Orifice, which is a program that allows people full access to your computer. They can mess with your files, control your Webcam (if you have one) so that they can see your every move, they can read your emails - the list is endless. The only way you can be affected by Back Orifice (or similar programs) is if somebody installs the software on your computer - or if you install software from an untrustworthy source, which is actually Back Orifice in disguise (this sometimes happens in Newsgroups). Back Orifice isn't a virus, but it can cause just as much damage (if not more!). Don't be paranoid about it, it isn't very common, but be careful who has access to your PC, and make sure you have good Virus and Trojan protection.

However, there are some serious security issues that affect everybody. One important thing to remember is to never send your credit card information over the Net unless you are sending it through a secure server. Secure sites use encryption, in conjunction with your browser, to ensure that any data sent is encoded and useless to hackers. Most Web browsers will alert you if the site you are visiting is secure. That also means that you shouldn't email your credit card information to anyone!

Also, it's important to ensure you never, ever give your ISP password to anybody. Many would-be 'hackers' (usually tubby American schoolboys) send emails to people pretending to represent somebody from the ISP. They ask for everyone to send their passwords for 'testing'. No ISP would ever do this, so don't be taken in. This risk is increased if you're using a content provider instead of an ISP. Many people take users of AOL, WebTV or CompuServe to be a bit gullible. This obviously isn't true, but they may be slightly less computer literate, making them the target for misguided kids the world over.

Harassment

Harassment online is rare, but it does happen occasionally. There have been one or two cases of Internet Stalking and there are some annoying people online that delight in upsetting others. Apparently it's illegal to drag these people from their houses and slap their chops, but they can be kicked off their ISPs, and reported to the police. In many cases, emails can be traced to the sender, even if they use forged addresses.

Don't be discouraged though, harassment is very rare, and can usually be sorted out simply by changing your email address. Your ISP should be able to do that for you for no charge. Failing that, change your ISP.

So, now you know what the Internet's all about, you'll probably want to connect as soon as possible. Thankfully, that's a lot simpler than you might think. In a few minutes, you could be sending your first email.

2-Getting Connected

What is needed to connect?

If you're not already on the Internet, there are a few things you'll need: a computer, a modem, and the correct software.

A modem (which stands for Modulator - Demodulator) is the piece of hardware which allows your computer to talk to other computers over the phone lines. It turns all of the beeps and squeals which are transmitted over the phone lines into binary information that your computer can understand. They have a plug in the back so that you can insert a normal phone cord. You may have to get an extension cable if your computer is situated any major distance from a phone socket. Modems are usually supplied with computers in this day and age, but if you're not sure, take a look. They take the form of either a small box which sits next to (or on top of) your computer, or cards which slot inside. If you have an internal card, you'll notice the slot in the back of your PC to accept a phone cable. Modems can be picked up for around £50 - though it may be worth investing in a more expensive one such as a Supra Express or Diamond model. The problem is that cheaper modems are often not BT approved, and this can mean endless problems. These include poor speed, failed connections, unrecognised 'busy line' tones, and a failure to realise when somebody is using the phone on the same line - it's just not worth it. The extra money generally buys you a faster and more reliable connection.

56k means that it can transfer, in theory, 56 thousand characters of text per second, or 5.6 kilobytes per second. You should remember that it can only receive data at this speed, whereas it will send at a maximum of 33.6k. So, if you're browsing a Web site, everything will download at 56k - but if you are sending emails or uploading files, it will only run at 33.6k. This is down to the special methods used to transfer the data at such high speeds. Nicer modems, with built in answering machines or pretty flashing lights can cost up to £200. You'd want to be sure it's compliant with the V90 standard, though. The V90 standard is a universally agreed one which ensures compatibility throughout the various brands. To begin with there were two different standards - 56k Flex and x2. Many ISPs refused to support 56k modems until a standard was agreed, and many 56k modems were shipped with 'flash roms'. These are chips which can be upgraded with new software - so that x2 and 56k Flex modems can now be upgraded to the V90 standard.

Slower modems are fine for many uses. They can be picked up second hand for as little as £10 - £15. Unless you download lots of big files, slower modems can be good buys, but you should always keep in mind that quicker modems may save you money in the long run, as long as you have to pay for local calls. Therefore you could consider a 28.8K modem.

If you want a really nippy connection, you have several options. For the home user, these are limited to ISDN and ADSL. ISDN (Integrated Standard Digital Network) offers a 10 bit connection, so it can download at 10 bytes per second. The bonus is that it comes with two lines, so you can be on the phone and on the Net at the same time. You can even use both lines for the Internet if you want, and download at up to 128k!

ADSL (Asymmetric Digital Subscriber Line) is a different kettle of fish. It's a newer technology that allows downloads at speeds of up to 200 kilobytes a second. This may be 'throttled' to 50-odd kilobytes a second for home usage, but that's incredibly fast. It's 'always-on' so you don't have any phonebill either. It's probably going to cost somewhere around £50 a month for home users, and an additional installation charge will also exist. You'll need a new type of modem too, but the advantages to heavy Internet users are tremendous. ADSL is only available in several major cities (such as London) right now, but it's thought that it'll be available all around the country by 2002.

Cable modems will become an option towards the end of the year, in some parts of the UK. They work via the same kinds of cable used to pump extra TV channels and phone lines into homes. However, little is known about the costs or specifications at the present time.

In terms of the computer you'll need, well, almost any computer can connect to the Internet. You could use a PC running any version of Windows, or Linux, a Mac, or even an Amiga. Macs are very well supported, and although an old machine, Amigas still have some support when it comes to Internet software. PCs are considered to be the real standard, but Macs are not too far behind. The bottom line is, if your computer was made within the past five years, you should have no problem whatsoever when it comes to connecting to the Internet.

Most modems connect to a COM port. All you need to do is turn off your computer, locate the slot (you may have two or more - it doesn't matter which you choose), and plug it in. When you switch on, so long as you're using Windows, the modem will automatically be detected and configured. In many cases you will need to insert a disk from the manufacturer which contains the drivers. Drivers are needed so that the computer knows how to talk to the modem. Windows contains standard drivers which will work with most modems, but recent models may have problems. If you don't have drivers, then most 56k modems will work OK, but only in 33.6k mode.

How to get Connected

There are various different ways of connecting to the Internet. The best ways for home users are either Online Services or Internet Service Providers.

Online Services

Online services include AOL and CompuServe. They supply not only Internet access, but their own exclusive content. This content is usually made up of pages, similar to the World Wide Web.

Many of them charge subscription fees, but they are suited more to those who have no previous Internet experience. They can be limiting - there are lots of Web pages that don't work with online services, and a lot of Internet software will experience problems. However, if you can afford it, you might find that the ease of use and friendly approach are more suitable for you. Once you've been online for a while, you may find that you need a little bit more freedom, and this is provided by the standard ISPs.

Internet Service Providers

Internet Service Providers (ISPs) have been around since the 1980s. One of the first in the UK was Demon (http://www.demon.co.uk), which is still going from strength to strength today. It is easy enough to get yourself up and running with an ISP, and enjoy the sort of freedom that some Online Services don't provide. The big advantage is that most of the decent ones are free.

Most of the free ISPs make money in two ways. Firstly, although you are paying no more for your phone call, the Phone Company pays some of the money from the call to the ISP. Also, the ISP charges quite large amounts for customer support. Some charge up to £1 per minute. However, it's very unlikely you'll ever need to use customer support, because they make everything so simple for you. Don't ever subscribe to a pay ISP unless you are particularly desperate to deal with a certain provider. There are no advantages and you're just wasting money. Expensive ISPs and Online Services get huge amounts of users by preying on beginners.

Recently, several companies have sprung up which offer completely free access - and even free phone calls. Far and away the best of these companies is Callnet 0800. They offer completely free access to the Internet 24 hours a day, on a freephone 0800 number. Several others, including IC24 and X-Stream also offer free access, though it is considerably more limited. Let's have a closer look at these ISPs (and several local call rate ones).

FreeServe

http://www.freeserve.co.uk

Cost per month: Free, excluding phone charges. Tech support costs 50p per minute.

Web Space: 5 Megs

FreeServe is the service operated by the Dixons group. All you need to do to sign on is to go into your local Dixons or Currys shop and get a free CD. FreeServe is well put together, but can prove difficult to remove from your PC. It is one of the biggest free ISPs out there, and helped to kick off the whole free ISP movement in the UK. Commendable indeed.

Demon

http://www.demon.net

Cost per month: £11.75, excluding phone charges.

Web Space: 20 Megs

Demon is a well established ISP (one of the first in the UK), and it's still attracting many visitors. One of the few ISPs to offer a fixed IP address. This is useful for some users, but for most offers nothing extra.

UK Online

http://www.ukonline.co.uk

Cost per month: Free, excluding phone charges. Support costs 25p/min, or £4.70 for unlimited support on lo-call number.

Web Space: Unlimited

UK Online was the first ISP to offer total UK coverage at local call rates, and also the first to offer unlimited amounts of Web space. Unlimited Web space for free? It's madness. EasyNet provide the speedy backbone.

AOL

http://www.aol.co.uk

Cost per month: £9.99 & 1p per minute - No phone charges.

Web Space: 10 Megs

AOL are famous for posting out CDs to people (probably the reason they have so many subscribers). They provide a reasonable service, but the use of AOL (like with any content provider) is restrictive compared to that provided by one of the normal ISPs. However, they do have a scheme in operation whereby it only costs 1p per minute to connect to them, day or night. This is helpful to those that spend a lot of time online during peak times. Heavy users should consider Clara (page 23) though.

Eidosnet

http://www.eidosnet.co.uk

Cost per month: Free.

Web Space: 20 Megs

Eidosnet is primarily a games players ISP. Using Eidosnet you have access to their games-playing server, as well as the Internet. Like UK Online, it uses

EasyNet for its backbone connection to the Internet, so you're guaranteed a speedy connection.

Callnet 0800

http://www.callnet0800.com

Cost per month: Free, no phone charges.

Webspace: 20 Megs

Callnet 0800 are a bit of an anomaly. They offer free, unlimited Internet access on an 0800 number. There's no catch and no obligation to spend any money. The only thing they demand is that you sign up to use their 145 telephone scheme. All that means is that you can dial 145 before making any phonecalls, and you'll save 30% over the standard BT rates. These phonecalls are then charged to your credit card. There's no obligation to use it, but you'd be mad not to.

New registrants are now charged £19.99 for a small device which plugs in between your phone and the socket. It simply re-routes your calls through Callnet Telecom automatically (without you having to dial 145 first). Users get the £19.99 back as a credit on their phone bill.

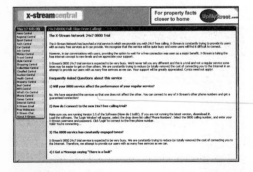

X-Stream

http://www.x-stream.co.uk

Cost per month: Free, excluding phone charges. Some free phonecalls.

Webspace: None.

X-Stream are a fairly well known free ISP. They are however famous for incredibly poor speeds and constant engaged tones, but they do offer 0800 access on some weekends. They have also been running a 24/7 0800 Internet trial lately, but reports are that it's very, very difficult to connect. You also have to put up with an advertising bar across your screen.

ClaraNet

http://www.clara.net

Cost per month: £6.99, 1p phonecalls.

Webspace: 50 Megs

Clara's deal is great for those that use the Internet a lot during peak times. Calls cost 1p/min all day long, which is a saving of up to 75% on BT rates. Calls are charged to your credit card. Clara offer a great mix of quality and value.

Madasafish

http://www.madasafish.com

Cost per month: Free, excluding phone charges.

Webspace: Unlimited

If you want a classy, polished ISP experience then you could certainly consider Madasafish, which provides a decent portal to the Internet and works at a good pace. You can also have as many email addresses as you like.

BT Internet

http://www.btinternet.co.uk

Cost per month: £9.99, lots of free phonecalls

Webspace: 2 GB

Completely free Internet access all weekday evenings and all the weekend. You also get unlimited email adresses and connection to Wireplay. One great service for online games players.

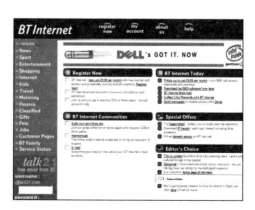

Totalise

http://www.totalise.net

Cost per month: Free, excluding phone charges.

Webspace: 20 Megs

Totalise were the first of a string of ISPS to offer free shares to users. The more you use it, the more shares you'll earn. We've heard of several heavy users with hundreds of pounds worth of shares, and the service isn't too bad either.

Other ISPs are run by such big-brands as BT Internet (http://www.btinternet.com), Yahoo! (http://www.yahoo.co.uk), WH Smith (http://www.whsmith.co.uk), Sainsbury (http://www.sainsbury.co.uk), Tesco (http://www.tesco.net), Virgin (http://www.virgin.net) and Granada(http://www.g-whizz.net), though they're all much of a muchness. Each is pretty much identical to the other, though they will perhaps offer some specific services or news updates tailored to reach their specific audiences.

The price of using the Internet

The cost of Net use varies a lot. It can be free (in the case of Callnet0800), it can be cheap (a la ClaraNet), or it can be costly (like Demon). You have to really keep on top of the latest news if you want to get the cheapest and best access. Always check sites such as The Matrix (http://www.thematrix.org.uk), or The Register (http://www.theregister.co.uk) for news. It could save you hundreds, or even thousands of pounds. If you want to sign up with a pay ISP (and to be honest, there doesn't seem much point any more), you can have a look through the various adverts in Internet magazines. The usual cost is around £10 per month. Beware of ISPs which charge by the minute. It is incredible that anyone actually wants to sign up with such services, when it's all available for free. Always be sure what you're signing up for, and don't be taken in by promises of so many hours of free access. With ISPs, the old 'you get what you pay for' maxim really does not apply. By selecting a free ISP, you can get more than some pay ISPs provide.

How to Connect

If you want to connect to an ISP, in 99.9% of cases the company in question will provide a CD full of software. Just put the CD in the drive and everything should be totally automated. However, in some cases (particularly with smaller ISPs) you may need to set things up manually. Eidosnet, at the time of writing, requires you to fill out some forms on their Website (http://www.eidosnet.co.uk). They then provide you with all of the information you need to connect. In order to get this information onto a PC, you need to follow these simple instructions.

1) Click on the start menu, then setting/control panels. Open 'Add/Remove Programs', and click the 'Windows Setup' tab. Double click on 'communications', and make sure 'Dial up Networking' is ticked. Then click OK twice. You may be asked to insert your Win95 CD. Follow all instructions, and then:

2) Double click on 'My Computer'.

3) Open the 'Dial-Up Networking' folder

4) Double click 'Make New Connection'

From here, it's quite simple. You're asked a number of questions about what hardware to use, and the phone number. Where it asks you to put the phone number, it's usually better to put the entire number, including the area code, into the 'Telephone Number' field, ignoring the 'area code' one. Once you've finished this, you should drag the new Icon onto the desktop. It won't let you move it, but it will create a short-cut, which is a big time saver. Then, when you need to connect to the Internet, you just double click the shortcut, and fill out the 'login' and 'password' fields. You can usually click the 'save password' tab, so that you don't have to enter your information every time you want to log on. However, this doesn't usually work if you have multiple login names on your PC (i.e. different settings for everybody who uses the computer).

ISDN

At the moment, ISDN (Integrated Services Digital Network) is an expensive way to access the Internet, but it's getting cheaper. The main reason that you would want to use ISDN is the speed increase gained over traditional analogue connections. ISDN uses digital signals, and can work at various speeds, depending on how much you want to spend. Phone bills can go sky-high if you want to use ISDN, and the line rental costs are high. However, a number of free ISPs support ISDN connections at no extra cost. It used to be the case that some ISPs charged absolutely outrageous prices for ISDN connections. Thankfully, that is all in the past. It might be worth waiting a while for the other forms of speedy Internet access which may soon become available. Amongst these are Internet delivery through the power lines, and modem/satellite connections (which are already available, to an extent).

The problem is, online technology is changing a lot quicker than the transmission medium - modem speeds change very slowly, but on the Web progress never stops. It was only four or five years ago that most Websites were on a grey background, with a few small images here and there. Now you've got huge images, Shockwave, Real Audio, Real Video, animated gifs - the next leap upwards in the speed stakes will have to be a large one.

The Web Browser

Web Browsers are pretty much a necessity if you want to use the Internet. They are the programs which allow you to see all of those World Wide Web pages. There are plenty of choices, but there are only three that really matter. Your ISP will probably supply you with a browser (most often this is Internet Explorer), but you may wish to try one of the alternatives.

Netscape

http://www.netscape.com

Netscape Navigator has been around for years, having been originally developed from the archaic browser Mosaic. For a long time it wasn't free, with only time-limited beta versions being free to use. However, when competition in the form of Internet Explorer came along, Netscape soon became a freebie. It's probably the best browser available. Very user friendly, and with full email and Newsgroup support, Netscape is one of the best options available.

Internet Explorer

http://www.microsoft.com/ie/

Early versions of Internet Explorer were pretty dire, but recent versions have become pretty good. It provides Email and Newsgroup support through external software, and has become very popular in the past two years. IE (as it is known) has become the most-used Internet software, but seeing that it's been given away with Windows, this is hardly surprising.

Opera
http://www.opera.no
Opera is an oddity - a browser that you have to pay for. Opera claims to be the smallest browser available, which uses a very small amount of memory and hard-disk space. This is quite different to the memory and system resource hogs that are IE and Netscape, and this makes Opera a good choice for people that can't afford to upgrade their old 486 PCs. It runs quickly even with slow processors, but it does cost money (around $35) which is a major drawback. Time limited demos are available.

Troubleshooting
There's not as much to go wrong when connecting to the Internet as you might think. With a small amount of luck, you should connect first time. The main problems you can experience are hardware ones. Broken modems can cause a lot of confusion. The first thing to do if you cannot connect with your ISP is to check all of the cables. Make sure the modem is connected properly to the computer, and that the phone cable is connected both to a phone terminal and the modem. This may sound like common sense, but you would be amazed at the amount of 'computer problems' that can be solved simply by checking connections.

If you still get problems connecting, you would be best advised to phone technical support. There are many things it could be, from problems at the ISP to incorrect dial up networking settings.

What else will I need?
Aside from the Web Browser, mentioned above, you'll certainly need an Email client (you can use the one included with your browser, if you like). There are plenty to choose from, as you can see in the Email section on page 42. Also, you will probably need a copy of WinZip (or any other kind of Zip software). WinZip is a piece of archiving software. It can compress and decompress files for transferring over the Internet. It's always best to compress large files when sending them over the Internet, because it can save a lot of time, and hence money. WinZip can often compress files by up to 50%, so you could send a reasonably large file in five minutes rather than ten. There are some files that shouldn't

be zipped. These include JPEG pictures, and AVI and MPEG movie files. They shouldn't be zipped because they're already compressed, and zipping could even increase their size. Once the file has reached its destination, it can be decompressed with WinZip. You can download WinZip from http://www.winzip.com.

You are advised to buy a decent Internet magazine that comes with a cover CD. These usually include all of the latest software on a regular basis, which can save you hours of downloading time.

If you don't already have one, you might also want a Telnet client. Telnet is a piece of software that allows you to remotely use another computer, using text commands. This is very useful for accessing chat programs (talkers) or accounts that you might have on UNIX machines. Windows comes with Telnet built in. To run it go to the start menu, select 'Run...' and type 'Telnet'. Mac users should get the latest version of NCSA Telnet.

3-Surfing the Web

Everyone has heard of 'surfing the Web' and 'cruising the Information Superhighway', but what does this mean? Of course, it's just one of those tired overused phrases that doesn't mean much. The World Wide Web (named by its English creator, Tim Berners-Lee) is the simplest and most user-friendly aspect of the Internet - and that really is saying something. If you're capable of moving a mouse around and pressing a few buttons, then you have the skills necessary to use the Web. These days, almost every part of the Internet revolves more or less around your Web browser - and once you've 'surfed the Web', you'll know what all the fuss is about.

The Make-up of a Web Page

NETSCAPE
The picture below shows a typical Web page displayed in Netscape.

The main features are:
1) 'Back' button. Clicking this will take you back to the previous Web page you were visiting.
2) 'Forward' button. Takes you forwards one page (works only if you've already used the back button).
3) 'Reload' button. If a page has failed to load or has loaded incorrectly, reloading can often help.
4) 'Home' button. Takes you to the page that you have told Netscape is your 'home page' (see below).
5) 'Search' button. Takes you to a search-engine page on Netscape's Web site.
6) 'My Netscape'. Takes you to a personalised page on the Netscape Web site.
7) 'Print' button. Allows you to print out the current Web page.
8) 'Security' button. Gives you all of the security information about the current page or site.
9) 'Stop' button. For use if you want the browser to stop loading a Web page.
10) 'Netscape' button. Takes you to the Netscape homepage. Most other browsers have similar buttons.
11) Bookmarks - Explained below.
12) Location. The address of the Web page currently being visited.
13) 'What's Related?' button. Suggests pages that contain similar content.
14) Personal Toolbar. You can specify certain bookmarks to appear on this bar, for easy access.
15) The actual Web Page window. Anything contained within this window is the Web site.
16) The Status Bar. Explained below.
17) The program segment icons. Click on these to go to the browser, mail, news or page editing windows.

Close up of the top bar.

INTERNET EXPLORER

The picture below shows a typical Web page displayed in Explorer.

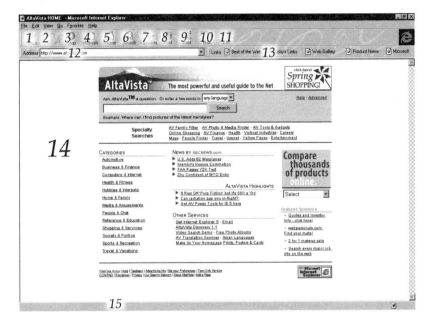

The main features are:

1) 'Back' button. Clicking this will take you back to the previous Web page you were visiting.

2) 'Forward' button. Takes you forwards one page (works only if you've already used the back button).

3) 'Stop' button. Stops a page from loading.

4) 'Refresh' button. If a page has failed to load or has loaded incorrectly, reloading can often help.

5) 'Home' button. Takes you to the page that you have told Explorer is your 'home page' (see below).

6) 'Search' button. Takes you to a search-engine page on Explorer's Web site.

7) 'Favourites'. The equivalent of Netscape's 'Bookmarks'.

8) 'Print' Button. Prints out the current Web site.

9) 'Font' button. Cycles through the various text styles available, so that you can pick one you're comfortable with.

3 1

10) 'Mail' button. Loads your chosen mail application.
11) 'Edit' button. For editing your own Web sites.
12) Address. The address of the Web page currently being visited.
13) A selection of links that Microsoft think you'll want to visit.
14) The actual Web Page window. Anything contained within this window is the Website
15) The Status Bar. See below.

As you can see, both browsers are pretty similar. Other browsers also share the same main characteristics, but many will have small cosmetic changes.

Home Pages

Not long ago, the Netscape Web site was the most visited site in the world, but not just for the reasons you might think. Netscape's browsers have always been programmed to visit the Netscape Web site when loaded. This is because http://www.netscape.com is the default (or home) page. You can however change this to be whatever you like. For example, you could set a news site to be your homepage. For example the Guardian homepage (http://www.guardian.co.uk) or the CNN site (http://www.cnn.com). It is also worth considering search engines such as Yahoo and Excite. These allow you to personalise your homepage by deciding which weather forecast and news stories to show. Whatever you decide it is useful to pick a site which is constantly updated, then every time you log on you will first have all the latest news and information. To change the homepage in Netscape, go to Preferences, then click 'Navigator' and change 'http://www.netscape.com' to your chosen site. On Internet Explorer, go to 'Internet Options' in the Tools menu.

Bookmarks/Favourites

Bookmarks, or Favourites (we'll call them bookmarks for the sake of argument) are a way of making sure you can always access your favourite sites. Let's say you've just found a site which you'd like to come back to in the future. All you need to do is to click the 'bookmarks' button, and select 'add bookmark'. Then the site will be added to a permanent list. You can rearrange or delete sites on the bookmarks list, and you can also sort the sites into folders. This way, you can store a list of hundreds of different Web sites, and easily find the one you're looking for.

The Status Bar

The status bar is a small, but important part of a browser. If you move the mouse over a link, the status bar will contain the location of the page or file to which the link points.

So, let's say you hold the cursor over a link which leads to AltaVista. The status bar will probably read 'http://www.altavista.com'. However, links can be made to put other words into the status bar. Using the same example, the status bar could be made to print the words 'Go to AltaVista!', instead of the actual address. This process can be used to send you to a site you did not wish to go to.

How to use a Web Browser

All Web browsers work in a pretty much identical way. Although the previous diagrams dealt with Netscape and Explorer they all have a row of buttons along the top, and an address field above or below them. The main section of the browser window displays the Web site you are currently visiting.

So, to begin with, connect to the Internet and load up your browser. Click in the text field at the top of the window, delete any text that is already in it, and type the following into in its place and press enter:

http://www.yahoo.co.uk

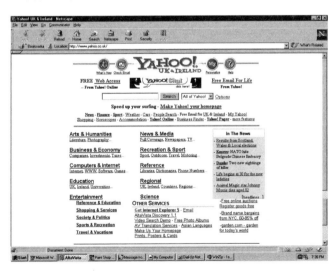

Congratulations, you've just visited your first Web site. Or at least, you should have if everything is working correctly. The HTTP part of that address is the part that tells your browser that the page you want to visit is a Web site. If you wanted to visit an FTP site, the HTTP section would be replaced by FTP://. The site you have just been directed to is Yahoo UK, a famous Web directory. By typing one of your interests into the 'search' field in the top of the Website window, and then clicking 'search', you can find a list of the sites which may interest you. Try the different features on the page and see how it all works. When you're finished, type http://www.yahoo.co.uk into the top field again, which will bring you back to the main page.

Now replace that address with http://www.altavista.com. AltaVista is a similar search site, but it works in a slightly different way. It is indifferent to the content of the sites it includes (the sites listed in Yahoo are hand-picked). It simply trawls its way through the Internet, listing each and every site which it comes across. As a result, it has tens of millions of Web pages for you to search through. Before you use it, however, try pressing the 'back' button at the top of your browser. You'll notice that this takes you back to the Yahoo page. Press the 'forward' button, and you go back to AltaVista. Simple isn't it?

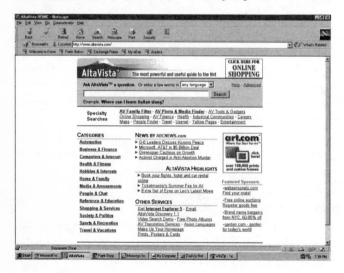

A little about Web Addresses

Now that you have dealt with Web Addresses, or URLs (Universal Resource Locators), you should know how they're made up. It's actually quite simple:

Example: http://www.altavista.com/index.html

http:// This shows that the destination is a Web site
www.altavista.com This is the name of the computer (see the previous chapter).
/index.html The page or file being viewed.

index.html is usually the main page of any site. If you go to any site, you will normally be transported to a file called index.html. This is true of top level sites (such as http://www.altavista.com/) or sites which reside in an individual folder (http://www.xe.net/currency/). You don't need to type index.html on the end of an address though, since it is the default file sent to you.

You should always remember that Web addresses are case sensitive, (upper and lower case letters are not seen as the same). If you use a different case, it just won't work.

Links and Buttons

The Web is made up of a huge amount of pages, all of which are joined together by links. A link is a word, picture or phrase that links to another file on the Web, usually another page or a picture. On AltaVista, for example, take the word 'help', to the right of the search field. This is a typical link, because it is in blue. Blue text usually, but not always, designates a link. If you hold the mouse cursor over a piece of text, then you can use the status bar (see below) to see if it's a link, and if it is, where it links to. When you click on the link, you are immediately transported to the linked file.

Have a play with AltaVista and using the back and forward buttons. You'll soon get the hang of it.

History Files & the Cache

All browsers retain a history, or list, of the sites you've visited. This way the browser can see if you've visited a site before, and can load the appropriate files from the cache. The cache is an amount of disk space (usually up to around 20 megabytes) where all of the Web pages and associated pictures that you have downloaded are stored. Your Web browser will refer to these files on disk to save downloading the same file time after time. So for example you may visit a site quite often that contains several large pictures. Your browser will store these large pictures in the cache and load them from disk each time you re-visit the site. This can save a lot of time and hassle. Most browsers offer a number of options concerning the cache. Largely these determine how often sites are 'refreshed'. It wouldn't be very good if you visited a news site which was only being loaded from the cache. You could be mistaken for believing that the site was a bit behind. Thankfully, clicking the 'refresh' button will re-download the entire site. It's probably advisable to instruct your browser to reload the page once per session.

You should be warned that the cache and history files can be used to spy on your Web activity. Netscape's history file isn't really readable without special spying software, but the cache is open to investigation, and the latest sites you've visited can be easily seen by prying eyes.

If you think somebody else might be wanting to find out about your browsing habits, then you can always flush the cache. This can be done from within the options page of your browser. If you're paranoid, then you can delete the history file too. In Netscape, this means deleting a file called 'netscape.hst', contained in the same folder as the Netscape executable (PC users can try c:\program files\netscape\program\netscape.hst). The History file in Internet Explorer can be removed by selecting *Tools*, then *Internet Options*, and then clicking *Clear History*.

Image Maps

Image maps are pictures which contain links. For example, you could have a map of the world, and clicking on each country would transport you to a page about that country. Image maps are frequently used on commercial sites, but they aren't used so much on personal Web sites, because they are notoriously hard to create without the right software. You can tell if a picture is an image map by moving the cursor around and watching the status bar. If the status bar shows any activity, then the picture is an image map.

Saving Files

It's likely that you'll regularly come across pages or pictures that you want to save. On a PC if it's a picture you want, all you need to do is click your right mouse button on the image, and go to 'Save As'. Then just save it wherever you like. If it's a Web page that you want, then all you need to do is go to the 'Save As' choice in the file menu. If it's a movie or sound file, you can just right click on the link which leads to the file, then select 'Save As', in the same way as if it were a picture. On a Mac you just need to drag the image outside the browser. Simple. Remember though that if you save a Web page, the pictures that go with it aren't automatically saved too. See 'off-line browsing' for more information about saving entire Web sites.

404 - Not found

It's infuriating, but often you'll follow what looks like a really interesting link, only to be greeted with a '404 - not found' error page. What this means is that the page or file no longer exists at that location. It could have been moved elsewhere, or it could simply have been deleted. There's no way around it, it is just plain annoying. Some search engines will re-visit links on their databases, and remove sites which contain 404 errors - but some are quicker to do this than others.

Search Engines & Directories

You should have already visited two of the main search engines in this chapter. They are very important as they are the means to finding what you want on the Net. Without them, you won't be able to do very much. Two of the best are AltaVista (http://www.altavista.com) and Yahoo (http://www.yahoo.co.uk). Yahoo is great in that all of the Web sites are sorted into categories, and are hand-picked. It's like a phone directory, but for the Internet. AltaVista is different in that it's an indiscriminate 'spider'. It automatically trawls the Web, and includes every page it finds in its database that relates to your search. It's the most complete search engine, but it can be harder to find exactly what you're looking for. Yahoo is good if you're looking for Websites on a general topic, but AltaVista is essential if you need to look for something specific. So, for example, if you want to look for a site concerning dogs, you'd go to Yahoo. If, however, you wanted information on how much to feed a particular breed, you'd go to AltaVista and enter a more detailed search term.

Yahoo is simple. You type in a word, click search, and it gives you the best categories to look in. If there's a lack of specific categories, it shows you the best individual site matches.

AltaVista is a different story. You type in a word, and it searches its database, bringing up all of the sites that contain that word in them. The more occurrences of the word, the higher up the list the site will be. You can search for both multiple words and sentences easily by using speech marks. So, for example if you wanted to search for some sites about Eastenders. You could try this search:

Eastenders soap "frank butcher"

This works quite well, and presents several good sites. No doubt you'd be able to work out some better ones yourself.

If you wanted to search for information about football, but weren't interested in American Football, you'd probably type:

Football -"american football"

Which tells AltaVista not to select pages that also contain the words "american football". On the other hand, you could just try typing 'soccer'. Virtually all search engines work in the same way, but most aren't as comprehensive as AltaVista. If you still fancy some variation, you could do worse than try the following:

Excite UK
http://www.excite.co.uk

Lycos UK
http://www.lycos.co.uk

HotBot
http://www.hotbot.com

UK Plus
http://www.ukplus.co.uk

Ask Jeeves
http://www.ask.co.uk

It takes time to get the best results from searching. Everybody seems to have their own methods of finding sites, which they all swear by. If you decide to stick with one search engine, always check out the 'Help' pages, which usually have some decent tips on using the service. Even if you think you know everything, you're still likely to find a few surprises.

Personalising

Some search sites (including, most notably, Yahoo) offer full personalisation. This means that you can set up a special version of the site as your homepage (so that it comes up whenever you load your browser). Yahoo offers possibly the best service. To start you need to select My Yahoo! (there is always a prominent link on the site). You can then choose what material to show whenever you visit the site. For example, you might want to be shown all of the latest news on your favourite football team, see what the top entertainment stories are, know the weather for wherever you like, or check out your stocks and shares or other financial news. Yahoo gives you the power to tailor its content to your own interests, and can be an excellent way of keeping one step ahead of the newspapers. You can have little applications on your page such as an exchange rate calculator based on up to the minute feeds of exchange rates. You can even list the top films and get a synopsis and a range of reviews on them by clicking their name. Other sites such as Deja.com (the Newsgroup archive service) and AltaVista offer similar services. Indeed, many other news related sites are starting to support these personalised portals, so you should notice them springing up all over the place.

By having much of the information you are interested in appear with up to the minute accuracy the second you log onto the Internet, you can save yourself a lot of time.

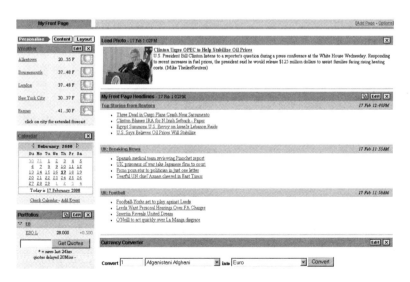

39

Multiple Search Engines

There are various ways of going through all of the search engines at once. One of the easiest is DogPile (http://www.dogpile.com).

It's a web-based search, you simply insert your word/s into the engine, and it piles up all of the results from all of the search engines it's aware of. Another way is to use one of the pieces of software especially developed for this task. One of these is WebFerret, which is available at http://www.ferretsoft.com/netferret/index.html. It certainly makes obscure searches a lot easier to manage.

Buying Online

The Web is more than just a magazine, it's also the world's biggest catalogue. Whatever you need to buy, you can probably find a Web site that allows you to get it. A lot of companies are only now waking up to the fact that there's money to be made through selling, and not just advertising things online. The most famous online shop, and the one by which all others are judged, has to be Amazon. It's the world's biggest bookshop, and they operate entirely through the Internet.

Amazon

http://www.amazon.co.uk

Amazon began life in the US, as Amazon.com. They have thousands of books in stock, and can order pretty much any title currently available. Amazon allows you not only to choose the books you want online, but pay for them online too. This is thanks to the use of a secure server. This encrypts your credit card information (and other stuff too) as it's sent to Amazon. Many people are sceptical of putting their credit card information online. This is why Amazon also provide the option of phoning them up with your number. Still, if you're brave enough, you can order books without ever leaving your PC. Amazon claim that nobody has ever suffered credit card fraud after having used their site - and with the level of security provided, this is easy to believe. It's just as safe as giving the information over the phone, if not safer.

Using Amazon is a simple affair. When you visit the site, you can see a small field into which you type your search words. This can be the name of the author, or the subject of the book you're looking for. When you click 'Go!', you'll be presented with a list of matching titles. You can then pick the ones that interest you. Often they have a further description or scan of the front of the book. If you find a book (or books) that you like, you can just add them to your virtual shopping basket. When you've got everything you need, you have to go to the virtual checkout. Then you just need to fill in some information (address, credit card information), and you're away. You should remember that there are postage costs to pay, but books on Amazon are often quite a lot cheaper than if you bought them in the high street. Price reductions are always stated, so you can make sure you're getting a good deal.

A recent competitor to Amazon is BOL (http://www.bol.com) which stands for Books Online. They've had a fairly vigorous advertising campaign and they offer an excellent service, but there's not much difference to make you choose between BOL and Amazon. Streets Online (http://www.infront.co.uk) have a books section too, which has some great bargains (their best sellers are all half price).

Online shops are springing up everywhere, and they sell just about everything. Thankfully, more and more are turning up here in the UK. Even supermarket chains are beginning to catch on, and for a small fee some chains will now deliver your online orders - see Sainsbury (http://www.sainsbury.co.uk) and Tesco (http://www.sainsbury.co.uk), for example.

Buying Smart

If you want to get the best bargains, you'll need to shop around. Or will you? Actually, no. Sites such as Chartdeals (http://www.chartdeals.co.uk) compile the prices of the top selling books, videos, games, CDs and DVDs. They clearly point out the cheapest dealer (including all postage & packing charges - what you see is what you pay), and you're always one click away from the best bargains. Continuously updated, ChartDeals is a much better proposition than checking each shopping site in turn.

Auctions

The online auction craze was started by eBay (http://www.ebay.com) several years ago. The idea came about when an American created a simple auction service for his wife to sell Pez dispensers. These days, you can buy everything on eBay. It acts as an intermediary between the buyers and the sellers. Anybody can bid or sell on eBay, and up to six million items are for sale on eBay at any time. It's mostly US-based, but any dealer with half a brain will also ship to the UK for a small extra cost.

Bidding in Dollars is easy - just make sure you know what the current exchange rate is, or check a Currency Converter (http://www.xe.net/currency/).

Unlike in conventional auctions, online auctions last for ages - usually five or seven days. Still, most bidding goes on in the last hour of the auction, as people try to put their bids in without pushing the price up prematurely.

Everything from comics and books to ancient gold and convertible sportscars can be found for auction at eBay, making it officially one of the most popular Websites in the world. It's really easy (and free) to register, and even easier to use. You bid for items based upon the maximum you're willing to pay - and from then on, eBay does the bidding for you (this is called Proxy Bidding). So, let's say you saw a book you wanted with a starting price of $3. If you were willing to pay $10 for it, you'd make a bid for $10, and, if you were the first bidder, the price would still be at $3. If someone else wanted the book and bid $6 for it, the price would rise to just above $6 - but you'd still be the high bidder. If someone else bid just over $10, you would no longer be the high bidder. For this reason, it's best to always bid just slightly higher than you want to - instead of bidding $10, make a bid of $10.20 to outfox people that would outbid you by one cent at the last minute!

eBay is truly excellent for people of all ages. You're even insured against fraud, though you're unlikely to be ripped off anyway. eBay has a great feedback system, where you can leave feedback (Positive, Neutral or Negative) about someone once you've finished a transaction with them. If you've had a good experience it's good manners to leave them a positive note, but if you're unhappy with the transaction, you can alert other eBayers as to the activities of the other party. Always be objective though, and don't start libelling people!

eBay is remarkably easy to use, and there are thousands of different categories. Once you've used it, you'll wonder how you ever lived without it. There is a UK version at http://www.ebay.co.uk, which also allows you to search the US site for items that can be shipped to England. This UK site is useful if you only wish to buy from sellers based in England, but probably more fuss if you are happy to buy from anywhere. Overall, the US site with a currency converter is the most convenient way of using eBay. See 'Buying from Abroad', on page 44.

UK auction sites also exist, though they're much, much quieter than eBay. The biggest site is QXL (http://www.qxl.co.uk), a massively publicised affair, which auctions off cheap electrical goods as well as holidays, collectables, and lots more. Users can run their own auctions, and lots are run by QXL themselves. It's a classy affair, and has a good reputation amongst buyers. It doesn't have the sheer range available on eBay, but it's useful if you'd rather keep your dealings based in the UK.

Another site of potential interest is Blue Cyle (http://www.bluecycle.com) which auctions off old items, including stolen goods which have been recovered. They have wide varieties of... well... 'interesting' goods for auction at any given time. When we had a peek, there were old cars, gold rings and even a pair of workmen's shovels, depicted by an awful, blurry picture taken by someone of the Kent constabulary. Wonderful.

Buying from Abroad

If you want to shop online, then there's a good chance you'll want to buy from another country at some point. Luckily, this is very easy. Larger stores will accept Credit Cards online, which is handy and safe - as long as they use a Secure Server. You can easily tell if their server is secure. On Netscape, the little padlock in the bottom left of your browser will be locked. Internet Explorer usually alerts you when you visit a secure site.

If the particular store doesn't accept online credit card transactions, see if they'll take telephone orders. This is an inconvenience because of the time differences and occasional language barriers. If all else fails, you'll probably have to send cash. This really isn't safe and the Post Office frown upon it, but it can be done. Cheques are also far less secure than cards. If it's an expensive item, you can look into the option of getting an International money order or something similar, but these cost in excess of £10 each.

Earning money online

There's money to be made, if you've got the time and inclination. One of the most popular ways at the moment is to sign up with AllAdvantage (http://www.alladvantage.com/). They offer money to anyone willing to put up with a small advertising bar at the bottom of their screen. The maximum money you can earn from your own surfing alone is about £7 per month, but the real money to be made is via referrals. If you refer somebody to the service, you'll get extra money each month, up to £1.20 per person. You also get money for the people that they refer, and all other referrals down three levels after that!

AllAdvantage are based in the US, and although earnings are calculated in dollars, you're paid in the form of a cheque made out in Pounds. Cheques are mailed out every month, as long as your earnings for that month equal around £12 or more.

If it sounds a bit like one of those awful MLM/Pyramid schemes, that's because it is quite a similar concept - except that AllAdvantage is proven to work. Some people make hundreds of pounds a month from this scheme. All for just surfing the Web like they usually do (and forcing all of their mates to sign up).

Another way to make some extra cash is to become a Webmaster, because there's also money to be made as an affiliate of one of the major Internet stores. Many, including Amazon, will allow you to link to their books and take a cut of the profit for each book sold directly through your link. The ideal way to use a scheme such as this is to incorporate it into a pre-existing Website.

Let's say you run a Website that is all about football. You could then create a little book review section, or even a dedicated bookshop section. There are plenty of books about football, so you could potentially earn a fair bit of money. Note, however, that more people will be likely to buy the books concerned if you appear knowledgeable, and it'll be especially useful if you provide full reviews of the books in question. Otherwise, the customer might as well skip you entirely and go straight to Amazon.

For details of the Amazon affiliate scheme, visit http://www.amazon.co.uk. Other sites, including WH Smiths Online (http://www.bookshop.co.uk) and Streets Online (http://www.infront.co.uk) run excellent affiliate schemes. They're worth checking out if you're serious about making a bit of extra money.

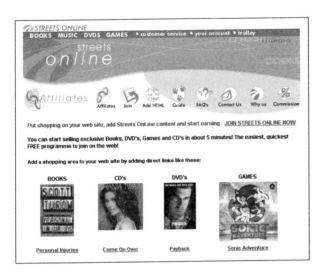

Using the Web to Download Software

The Internet is a great way of finding out about all of the latest software. Magazine cover-CDs are all well and good, but they can only contain a very small fraction of the latest shareware. You can get just about every shareware product in the world from the Internet.

There are several large directories of software.

The most famous ones of all are probably Shareware.com (http://www.shareware.com) and Download.com (http://www.download.com). They both have search engines that you can use to track down software. When you've found the program you want, it lets you download it from any of the sites that it has indexed. This way you can pick the site that is closest to you, for a quicker download.

Of course, you could also use a standard search engine to find software. Let's say you wanted a program that allows you to print disk labels. You could go to AltaVista, and type: '"print disk labels" shareware'

Another way of downloading software with your Web browser is via FTP, which stands for File Transfer Protocol, and is covered later on in this book (see page 67). You can use an FTP search engine, such as the one at http://ftpsearch.lycos.com to find the files you need - but this does mean that you will need to know the actual filename of the software you're looking for. You can't really generalise.

Plugins

Web Browsers work pretty well in their own right, but to get the greatest multimedia experience of them all, you'll need some plugins. They go inside a 'plug-ins' folder which is usually located inside your browser folder. When your browser loads, it checks this folder and uses the plugins to increase the different sorts of files that it can recognise and deal with.

The most famous plugins are those created by MacroMedia (http://www.macromedia.com). They allow you to run small programs, which are integrated into Web pages. These might take the form of animations or small games. Animations usually take a very long time to load into browsers, because of the huge amount of data that needs to be transferred to your browser. MacroMedia software can bypass this by storing the data in a very different (and highly compressed) way. Using MacroMedia plugins, you can get an animation to download and play in seconds, rather than minutes. Sound is also well supported - it can be 'streamed' from a Web site. This means it can play as it downloads. This is all done totally transparently, without any gaps or skipping in the sound (well... that's the theory). These programs are created using fairly expensive software, which is only really available to those who create professional Web sites. The plugins required to play the files are free, however.

Some browsers come with the proper plugins included, but if you don't have them, you can get them from MacroMedia's Web site. When you've got the right plugins, you should pay a visit to the funky Tizer Web site, at http://www.tizer.co.uk - it's a great example of how to use MacroMedia files.

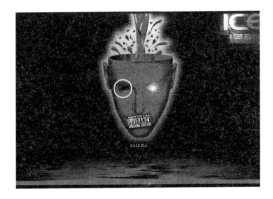

RealPlayer also provides a browser plugin - it's the most famous way of streaming audio and video over the Internet. You can use it to watch Korean daytime TV (no, seriously), or to listen to any of the hundreds of Radio stations which you can find on the Internet. Even Virgin radio is available online! See http://www.virginradio.co.uk/onair/listen.htm. The quality is mildly rubbish, but it's an amusing diversion. RealPlayer is available as a standalone program which is linked to your browser, but a small plugin is also provided. The plugin lets you run RealAudio or RealVideo content from your browser window, without the need to load the separate program. You can get RealPlayer for free from http://www.real.com.

Java

Java is basically a programming language. The catch point is that programs written in Java can be run on any platform that supports it. This is unlike standard computer software, which is written to run on only one platform. For example, PC software only works on PCs. Mac software does not work on a PC, and so on. Java eliminates these problems, but does so very slowly. The problem is that the software needed to interpret Java is quite heavy on system resources.

You need quite a powerful machine to use Java properly. There are a fair few Java programs available on the Web that will run through your browser, see 'True Interaction on the World Wide Web', on page 49 for a great example of this. However, Java has never really turned out to be the Big Thing that people had predicted. It's unreliable and slow. People have been hyping it since the dawn of time, but with a few novel exceptions, it's not worth the effort for the average Web user. Everyone's heard about it, and everyone will use it from time to time, but it's just not the ideal solution to the Web's problems. Java isn't to be confused with Javascript, which is somewhat different. Javascript is a useful scripting language, which makes Web pages more user friendly and doesn't slow things down. It also doesn't have to be separately downloaded, like Java. Java programs (or applets) run independently, but Javascript is translated by your browser.

Cookies

Cookies are small biscuits, which often contain nuts or chocolate chips. In the computer world, however, they are small files which contain personal information about you. They are usually used in a perfectly decent way. Let's say you visit a site which requires a login name or password. To save time, the site may allow you to use a cookie instead - so that it can identify you without you having to constantly retype the same information. The trouble is, they can also store information about your shopping habits, your top shelf collecting habits (should you have any), and what sorts of products you'd be interested in buying. Cookies are only visible to the people that have set them, they aren't just there for the world to see. However, many people are wary of using them. All browsers allow you to turn them off, so check out the options page of your chosen browser if you are scared of Big Brother.

Browser Settings

Browsers these days are pretty customisable. The main functions you may wish to change are those which affect the appearance of the browser. Fonts, for example. It can be useful to change the style or size of the text if you have problems with your vision, or just for a refreshing change. You can also change the colours of various text styles. This could mean making links red instead of blue, for example.

Also within the options pages of your browser, you can turn Java on and off. If you have a slow machine, it's probably best to turn it off, and only turn it back on when you know you're going to need it. Javascript should usually be left on, unless you find it has a tendency to crash your browser.

If you have a slow connection, or you're in a hurry, you might find it useful to turn off image loading. What this means is that the browser will only download Web pages, and not any of the images that come with them. This makes things a lot quicker in most cases. Browsers have a menu item or icon that allows you to load all of the images on the page.

Netscape has a section in its preferences page called 'Applications'. This is where Netscape works out how to use certain types of files. For example, if you click on a link that leads to an AVI (movie) file, it looks at the application's preferences to see what it should do with the file. It could be that you've told it to download the file then automatically play it using your favourite movie player. On the other hand, you could just get Netscape to bring up the 'save' dialogue, so that you can save it wherever you like. This section is best left well alone, unless you have a real reason to fiddle with it (and good instructions).

True interaction on the World Wide Web

If you want to really interact with something through the World Wide Web, then there can be little more bizarre than the Telegarden. Found at http://telegarden.aec.at/, the Telegarden allows you to plant and water seeds, using a robotic arm. You can keep track of your plants as they grow, and water them as if they were your own! It truly is Interaction at it's very best!

Also, you might want to try your hand at painting. The Puma Paint Project allows you to paint your masterpiece entirely over the Internet. You control a robotic arm which paints whatever you draw, using Java. Pretty amazing by anybody's standards. You can try it out for yourself at http://yugo.mme.wilkes.edu/~villanov/. You just have to be impressed.

Censorship

Yes, there are pictures of naked people on the Internet. There are also Nazis, the KKK and all other sorts of vile organisations. If you want to protect your children, then there are various options open to you. The best is to use a piece of software developed especially to block out pornography or violence. Two highly rated packages for the job are NetNanny (http://www.netnanny.com/) or Cybersitter (http://www.cybersitter.com/)

If, on the other hand, your Web access is being blocked or censored against your will, then you're advised to check out http://www.peacefire.org/ which has some good tips on getting around Web censorship. Assuming of course that access to that site itself is not being blocked out (as it frequently is).

Web-Based Email

Email is a handy thing to have, wherever you are in the world. Unfortunately, you can't always access your email if you're in another country. Very few ISPs have numbers you can call if you're outside the country. But hooray, thanks to Web based email, you can still carry on with your affairs without messing about with somebody else's email software. It works entirely through the Web, no messing about with POP addresses or anything. It's not just useful for those that travel a lot, it can also be used for an extra level of anonymity, or simply as an address to use when you post to Newsgroups.

For more information on Web based email, see the email chapter starting on page 52.

Off-line Browsing

You don't need to be online to view Web pages, but it helps. When off-line, you can view pages that you've downloaded previously. Using a piece of software such as Teleport Pro (http://www.tenmax.com) you can download whole Web sites, or parts of Web sites. Then you can browse them when not connected to the Internet. If you intend on reading the whole Web site, off-line reading is a lot less damaging to your phone bill. A fairly large site can be downloaded in about 10 minutes (or less), and you can be picky about the type of files downloaded (no large movie files, for example). To browse the site online and slowly read through it could take ages. Off-line browsing offers major benefits, especially if you're a student and you need to keep referring back to a site.

Anonymity

On the Internet, you have no true anonymity. If you visit a Web site, then somewhere in the world your IP address (and quite possibly more information) will be included in some logs. It'll list every file that you visited, and using this log, it would be possible to trace you (or the computer you used, at any rate). Unfortunately, that's just the way it is. There's no way of changing it. In these security-conscious days, logs are kept of just about everything. There's no real ways of keeping any sort of anonymity, but there are things you can do to make it difficult for people to trace you. Take, for example, the Anonymizer (http://www.anonymizer.org). Using this service, you can make sure that no logs are kept of your Web movements.

The basic idea is this: you prefix the Web address of the site you want to visit with an address given by the Anonymizer. So, if you wanted to visit Yahoo, you might type:

http://www.anonymizer.com:8080/http://www.yahoo.com

What would happen then, is that the Anonymizer server would fetch the page and then relay it to you. So in effect, you aren't actually visiting Yahoo, the Anonymizer is. The Anonymizer acts as a proxy server, but it keeps no logs of anything. This is the best way of protecting yourself, but theoretically someone could still be keeping up with what you're doing at the ISP end of things.

The Anonymizer is a pay service, but you can use it for free. There's just a delay between it receiving the page and then sending it to you. There's no delay if you want to pay. At the end of the day, if the Anonymizer isn't good enough for you (and it's not great), then you have to consider not bothering with the Internet. That's just the way it is.

Virus worries
Common sense is the best way forwards when it comes to virus concerns. You should always have a Virus checker running - and that means always! Never run a piece of software without having virus checked it, or at least check everything that doesn't come from a well known source. This pretty much applies to all forms of Internet activity, not just Web browsing. Check out http://www.norton.com or http://www.mcaffee.com for some good Virus checking software.

4-Email

What is Email?

Email has become by far the most popular and productive aspect of the Internet. It was in use long before the World Wide Web, and despite having changed very little over the past twenty years, it's gaining popularity every day.

It was initially only used by the military and university students, but now almost everybody with access to a computer has their own email account. Once you try it, you'll know why. Who couldn't find a use for an instant postal service? You click a button, and your message can be anywhere in the world within seconds. It's not limited to simple messages either, you can send images, programs, and spreadsheets - any sort of file you like, and it's a lot simpler than you might imagine. Faxing offers much the same kind of service, but it's slower and certainly a great deal more costly. No matter where you send an email it still costs only a few pence.

It's a great way of communicating, whether it's to friends, business contacts, or loved ones. It's so simple there can be few excuses for not having your own email address.

Your email address will probably take the form name@isp.com. The 'name' part is usually the same name you use to log onto the Internet. Any information on the other side of the @ is the address of the machine upon which your email is stored until you pick it up. Your ISP will have provided you with your email address.

What will you need?

The chances are, your Internet Service Provider has already given you a CD full of software to use with your Internet account. Usually this is either Internet Explorer (with the Outlook email program), or Netscape, with it's built in mailer. However, if you don't have an email program, or would like to try something different, then the following three programs are the most popular choices.

Eudora Lite or Eudora Pro

http://www.eudora.com

Price: Lite version: Free.

Eudora is a stand-alone email program which has become on of the world's favourites - and not without good reason. It has many, many powerful features, despite being very simple to master. For example, you can use it to automatically file messages from certain people into certain folders, or delete messages that contain certain phrases. It can be annoying receiving junk email, and Eudora is great at making sure you don't get bogged down with it all. Eudora has recently become freeware, for those willing to put up with a mildly intrusive advertising box in their mail window. If you still want to pay, however, the advertising goes away. Beware beta versions, which expire and refuse to work after a certain date, forcing you to upgrade. Grrr.

Netscape

http://www.netscape.com

Price: Free

Netscape has had email support for years. Unfortunately, it hasn't progressed a great deal in that time. It offers simplicity and convenience though, and it's unlikely that many people would need many more features than Netscape has to offer.

Outlook Express

http://www.microsoft.com/

Price: Free

Outlook is a kind of compromise between Eudora and Netscape. It's linked to Internet Explorer, so many people use it for convenience. It is a program in its own right though, and can be used in conjunction with any other browser. Compared to Microsoft's previous effort, Exchange, it is a real improvement. It can be a pain in the backside to set up, but because it's bundled with most PCs, many people us it. It's useful if you have more than one email account that needs checking regularly, since it can handle more than one a time, unlike Netscape.

Setting up

Setting up your email program is generally very easy. In most cases, the software provided by your ISP will already be set up for you. When using a different program however, you will need to get a few details from your ISP (or your previously set up mail software). If you lack any of the necessary information, then you can phone the support line of your

ISP, and they will be happy to give it to you (though they may not be able to supply your password over the phone). The same information will be needed whatever email software you use - and generally, you won't need to know anything else to get started. Any program specific information you need will be included in the documentation (often provided in the form of a text file, and not a printed manual).

You will need the following information to set up your mailer:

You will need to know the address of the mail server (this usually takes the form mail.isp.net - for example, if you're on Freeola, your mail server may be mail.freeola.net).

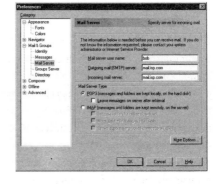

Your login name (usually the same name you use when dialling your ISP).

Your password (again, usually the same as the one used to log on with).

Your email address (usually login-name@isp)

You must enter these into the preferences screen of your chosen mailer. To get to the options screen of Netscape, select the 'Edit' menu, click on 'Preferences', click the 'Mail & Groups' tab, and fill out any of the applicable sections. On Eudora, go to the 'Tools' menu, and select 'Options'. Outlook should automatically bring up the options screen the first time you load it up. To set up another account in Outlook, go to the Tools menu, select Accounts/Add/Mail, and follow the wizard instructions. From then on, both email accounts will be checked when you click 'send and receive'. You can add as many accounts as you like.

Usually the 'Return Address' section can be left blank, since your email software usually fills this out for you. If you do need to fill it out, there is one thing you should remember. Although your mail server is mail.wherever.net, you don't write your email address as myname@mail.whatever.net, the .mail part is left out. So you would enter it as myname@whatever.net

Sending mail is extremely easy. Usually it means clicking the 'File' menu, and selecting 'New Message'. In Eudora you select the 'Message' menu and then 'New'. Whichever email program you have it will contain simple icons representing commonly used menu items. You simply click on these to activate them. Once you have the blank mail message on screen, all you need to do is place the address of the recipient in the 'To:' field, write your mail in the space provided, and click 'Send'. Some packages such as Outlook may need you to press the Send/Receive button as a final step. It's that simple. Emails can be of any length, within reason. You would be hard pushed to write an email that took up two megabytes of disk space.

With many email programs you can add HTML - the language used to create Web pages. So, for example, you could send an email with images, bold or underlined text, and links to Web sites. Many programs allow you to do this without any knowledge of HTML programming. Netscape, for example, includes many text formatting options in the 'Format' menu. Experiment with the different options, but be warned that many email-users may not be able to read emails that include HTML. They would see your text, but it would be surrounded by lots of extraneous characters. It's always best to ask before sending HTML email. Also, ensure that you never send email with HTML formatting to Newsgroups. It'll get you into trouble with the Newsgroup.

The CC (Carbon Copy) and BCC (Blind Carbon Copy) fields are for sending messages to more than one person. This can also be achieved in many programs simply by putting a comma or semicolon between the different addresses in the 'To:' field, but CC is still used, most often for internal business mail. BCC is the same, except that the recipients don't know who else has received the mail.

Sending Files

If you want to attach a file to your email, you can usually just select the file in Windows, and drag it into the mail window. All email programs also have an 'Attach' menu item or Icon too. The attach icon is usually a picture of a paper-clip. Make sure the file you're attaching isn't too huge though - most mail servers have certain restrictions on the size a mail can be (usually about two megabytes).

To send a file therefore:
1)   Load up your chosen software, and click the 'New Mail' icon, or select it from the menu.

2) Put the email address of the person you wish to contact in the 'to' field.
3) If there is an attach icon (usually represented by a paper-clip), then click it. If not, select 'attach file' from the menu, and find and select the file you wish to send. Alternatively, you can open the folder on your hard disk that contains the file, and then drag the file into the main text field of your current email.
4) Click 'Send'.

Now you'll notice that when you send your email, it will take much longer than usual. This is because the file needs to be uploaded to the email server first. Also, this means that it could take longer to reach its intended destination. You should always remember to ask somebody before sending them a large file. It can be irritating to have to wait ages whilst email downloads, especially when you don't know what it is, or who it's from. If you want to send the large file to more than one person, then simply add the extra names to the list of recipients. That way, the file need only be uploaded to the mailserver once. Also, you should be careful when sending executable files, because you could accidentally infect somebody's computer with a virus. You should always be careful about the programs people might send to you for the same reason. See the section concerning viruses for more information.

With a bit of luck, you should soon start to receive some emails. If you decide to reply to these, you can do so by either clicking the Reply icon, or selecting reply from the appropriate menu. When you do this you will get the standard mail-creation page, only this time it won't be blank. The correct address(es) should already be in place, and the mail to which you are replying will be quoted. This means that it will be displayed with a symbol at the start of each line. Usually this takes the form of either > or |. Most packages allow you to omit this original mail by crossing a box in the options menu, or simply deleting the old part of the message manually. It is however polite to include the quoted mail, at least partially, so that the recipient doesn't need to be reminded what it is you're talking about. You can then either put your new text at the top of the message, or you can write your comments interspersed amongst the quoted email. This can be good for saving time, and helping to avoid confusion.

Sometimes, you may receive emails that you would like to share with someone else. Usually these take the form of particularly bad jokes, secrets mailed to you by trusting friends, or business emails that you would like colleagues to see. If this is the case, all email programs worth their salt have the ability to forward email. It's very much like replying, but instead of the email going back to the sender, it can go wherever you like. The subject of a forwarded message generally begins with FWD: You can also add your own comments to the top of the mail if you want. Usually, to forward an email you must get the mail up on screen, and find the 'Forward' icon or menu item.

One of the good things about email is that you don't need to be online to write one out. You can be offline. All you need to do is load your choice of software, write out a nice long email, then only connect before you send it. This can cut down dramatically on phone bill charges, especially at peak times. This is especially useful if you frequent Newsgroups, as many Newsgroup readers are specifically designed for offline use (see page 67)

If you ever decide to change your email program, you might like to try and export your emails into your new browser. This can sometimes be done between some mail programs, including Eudora and Outlook. However, the process can be fraught with problems, so be sure to check the documentation before trying it.

If you are concerned about privacy, there are two main things to remember. Firstly, email is not secure. It would be relatively easy for someone to intercept anything you send over the Internet. So be careful what you say. Big brother does watch Internet communications, focusing in on specific words - like 'kill the PM', 'semtex', or 'foot-fetish'. You have been warned. Also, make sure that if you're using company-based email for non-company reasons, you're not leaving evidence of your communications in an 'outbox' folder. You must also ensure that the emails are then deleted from the 'trashcan' folder, if one exists. Many email programs keep all sent mails on the hard drive, and if someone is poking around on your computer, he or she could easily see everything that you've written to your friends or colleagues. Comments such as 'my boss is a nosey old duffer that reads my personal emails', presumably. On occasion people have lost their jobs because of situations such as these.

Freemail

If you have joined Freeserve, or any other free Internet service, you may not have been provided with a proper email address. Thankfully, as time goes on, more and more free providers are giving you a proper email address. Sometimes however, you are expected to use a free email service. These usually operate over the Web, but it's possible to find a free POP account (one that you use with a mail program), if you look hard enough.

Many people use Web based free email as a form of extra privacy protection. Whilst they are certainly not foolproof, they do provide an extra layer of protection which should help to hide your identity from all but the most determined madmen. If you want (almost) totally private email, you'll need to read the section about anonymous remailers, later in this chapter. Another potential reason to use a Web based email system is portability. You can check your email from any computer, anywhere in the world, without having to mess with server settings in a mail program you may not be used to. Useful especially to those forced into using Internet Cafes.

So, you want free Web based email? Here are the best choices open to you:

Yahoo! Mail

http://www.yahoo.co.uk

Yahoo offers a good, simple way of running a Web based email address. It can be better in the UK than HotMail, because it's usually considerably quicker. However, you might find it a little more daunting than HotMail if you are a total beginner. In reality, there is not much between the two.

HotMail

http://www.hotmail.com

Despite being owned by spooky megacorp Microsoft, HotMail is very good. It can mess you around in terms of speed at peak times, but you really can't go wrong with it. You can even send attachments in your emails, and post to Newsgroups. The HotMail Website contains detailed instructions

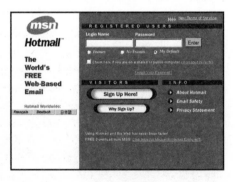

on signing up and using the service, but suffice it to say that it works in exactly the same way as conventional mail. Any email that you keep does not clog up your hardisk either.

We've only covered some of the bigger outfits above. The truth is, every man and his dog offers Web based email now. You can get it from just about any big Website you like, but they're all pretty much the same as one another. We advise sticking to Hotmail, because at least you can be sure that they'll be around for a while.

Organising your email

If you run a business, or even if you're just mightily popular, you may be interested in an address book. They can be very useful when it comes to arranging your addresses, and most mailers come with an address book built in. Netscape has one, which can be accessed from the 'communicator' menu. It works in the form of 'cards' for each entry. You can fill out all of the information you'd need on the card, and then easily search through your records to find certain words. It's just like a conventional address book, only searchable and more convenient. Similar functions are available whatever software you use.

Filtering email can be very useful at times. Filtering is a way of putting mail into a set place as it arrives. So, for example, you can get programs such as Eudora to look for the word 'earn cash quick' on all incoming emails, and delete any mails that match. If you're worried about filtering accidentally deleting your important emails, you can get your program to place the mail into a folder which you can manually empty at the end of each day or week. That way, you can just scan the subjects before you delete them. Eudora is by far the best option if filtering is important to you, and it really helps cut down on the amount of rubbish you are forced to read.

General tips

It's important to remember when sending emails that your mail will be read by a human being, and not a computer. Try and be polite and use good grammar. In some cases, particularly when contacting people you don't know, lazy emails can make you look a bit dense. Of course, it doesn't mean you are - but there are times when all you have to go on about a person are their emails - and making a good impression can be important. This is especially true when mailing for business or posting to Newsgroups. Of course, most Internet users are lazy enough, and resort to the common tactic of using strange abbreviations, not using correct grammar and leaving out all upper-case letters. This is fine - as long as the person you're sending them to will be able to understand them and you do not need to impress them.

One other way of saving time when sending emails is to use something called a signature. A signature (or .sig) is a small piece of text which your email program tags onto the end of any emails that you send. So, for example, you might want it to say something simple, like 'Regards, Ichabod'. You may want to include your postal address, if you use email for your business. On a personal note many people stick witty or interesting quotes in. It's entirely up to you. It's considered bad manners and a waste of Internet resources to include any more than five lines in your .sig, though. The details of setting up a signature will be outlined in the documentation provided with your choice of software.

Dealing with Spam

As well as being a very tasty canned meat product and a source of merriment for Monty Python fans, spam is also a word used to describe junk mail on the Internet. Don't be surprised if within a few weeks of using the Internet, you start to get loads of unsolicited junk in your inbox. You can liken junk mail on the Internet to junk mail that comes through your letterbox. You'll usually want to bin it immediately. The senders of junk email are a mixed bag of idiots and shady, though legitimate, companies. There are many different types of spam, but generally, they fit into one of three categories.

The most common is the old "$$$ GET CASH QUICK!" scheme, based around a pyramid scam. The idea is that you send $5 to everyone on the list, and then pass the list on with your name at the bottom, deleting the top entry and moving the others up. That way, as the reports circulate, you gain money. In theory. It doesn't work and is totally illegal. Obviously one for the bin.

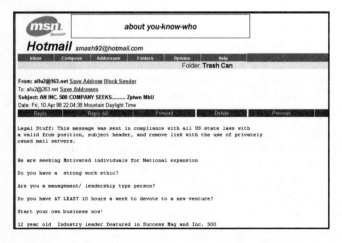

The second type is of the "See our girls NUDE!" variety. The Internet pornography industry loves to fill your inbox with promises of nudity, filth, and general depravity. This is unfortunate, since they never target their audiences, so children can just as likely end up getting it as anyone else. It's not really worth fretting over though, since they never post images, and rarely mention anything truly unpleasant in their advertising, but those of a sensitive disposition might like to invest in a program with email filtering capabilities.

The third type of spam is that which tries to sell you something. The general rule is that if you want to avoid being ripped off, do not buy anything from spammers.

One thing a lot of these spam mails contain is a small paragraph at the beginning, which usually reads something like this:

This e-mail message is being sent in accordance with proposed U.S. Federal regulations for commercial e-mail as well as the Washington state commercial e-mail law. For more information please see: http://www.wa.gov/wwweb/AGO/junkemail/ [Washington State Law].
Sender Information: Scum Industries, PO BOX 666, Nowhere Village, USA
To be removed from future promotions at no cost to you, email bubba@scum.com

Don't be fooled. A lot of spammers include this message to make it look as though they are running a completely respectable operation. Be very wary of emailing them and asking to be removed from their mailing lists. This can be just another way to harvest your email address. There is often a computer program sitting around waiting for you to send it a removal email, and when you do, it picks out your email address, and adds it to a list. Then at the end of the day, the spammer has a nice list of verified email addresses that he can sell to some other moron. Some companies have an honest removal option, but you have to decide if they are worth the risk. You rarely receive another email from the same person anyway.

So, how do these people get your email address in the first place? Unfortunately, that's quite simple. Firstly, if you make Newsgroup postings, then you will almost certainly get spam. Spammers have robots that constantly scan the Newsgroups, and steal all of the addresses that they can get their grubby little paws on. One way around this is to change the settings in your software. For example, in Netscape, you can alter the field which contains your email address. So, if you are bob@home.net, you can change it to read bob@goober.home.net. Of course, if somebody then sends you an email, it will not reach you. If you think people may want to reply via email, you can simply state in your posting that the 'goober' part will need to be removed from your address (as shown below). This is a pain though, because if you forget to put it right again, nobody will be able to reply to your emails. The solution to this is to use a standalone News program (see the

Newsgroups chapter on page 56). Also, ensure that you don't just insert the word 'nospam' into your email address, because those crafty spammers have worked out that 'nospam' is the most common insert into an address, and their latest software can simply remove it. Pick something different.

Another way in which the fiendish little devils can get your address is through unscrupulous companies. Many Web sites will ask for your email address for some reason, and there are a tiny minority that have no problem with selling your email address to spammers. This is why it helps to get a spare free email account to use when signing up for things over the Internet. There's no need to be paranoid though - most Web sites are perfectly trustworthy.

Video & Audio

For longer than it's possible to remember, people have been promising that we'll soon be communicating using video and audio messages (generally via a sophisticated wristwatch) instead of plain text emails. It hasn't really happened yet (mostly because normal modems are just too slow to make it worthwhile), but it's possible to do if you have the patience and the software.

Perhaps the best software is RealEncoder. You can get it from http://www.real.com, but be warned that it's not freeware. However, software to play the files is freely available from the same site, in the form of RealPlayer. RealEncoder can compress video and audio files to an almost unbelievable extent. You could easily compress a 30 second audio clip to about 55k - which would take about 15 seconds or less to send or receive. The quality wouldn't be brilliant, but it would be more than sufficient. Movie clips can also be compressed really well - a 25 second clip, with very good quality video and good sound can fit into 500k, which would take about 2 minutes to send or receive. Of course, you should never send files over about 100k without asking the recipient first.

Another audio option is MP3. You've probably heard in the news that many pop stars have been sending out press releases showing their mock-disgust at how MP3 is harming the music industry. It can squeeze audio files into incredibly small sizes without affecting the quality. You could take a track off CD, and store it in perfect CD quality stereo, and fit it into only 3 or 4 megabytes. You can't really go sending large files like that over email, but you could probably send an FM quality version, as long as you obtained the permission of the recipient beforehand. MP3 software is mostly shareware, too. Go to http://www.mp3.com for more information, or http://www.winamp.com for a great player. It's shareware, but it never expires. Make sure you pay for it if you use it a lot, because that's the only way it will continue to be developed.

There are numerous other ways of compressing video and audio into emails, but none are as well used as the above options. Always check before you send somebody a media file that they have the correct software needed to play it.

Mailing Lists

If you have a particular interest, you will probably find a mailing list for it. A mailing list is a good way of sharing an interest with like minded groups of people. In many ways it's a similar concept to that of a Newsgroup (see page 56). You can email a message to the server, and that message will be sent to everybody on the list. They are good for making announcements, or finding out the latest gossip. The amount of subjects range from soaps such as Eastenders & Coronation Street, to computer viruses, system administration, and so on. You can even set up your own mailing lists pretty easily, and for no cost. This is thanks to sites such as http://www.coollist.com, which support themselves by tagging advertising onto the postings. There are more complex ways of managing list servers, but they require that you have access to a machine running a form of the UNIX operating system and the technical knowledge that goes with it.

If you want to join a mailing list, then joining instructions are always provided. However, you should always keep the first mails that you get from the list, which provide removal instructions. You should always unsubscribe correctly from the list, not just send out a message to the entire group asking to be unsubscribed.

Some mailing lists are strictly one-way, and do not allow members of the list to make their own posts. These include, for example, Joke mailing lists (of which several hundred exist). Also, some lists are moderated. This means that all of the messages have to be read by the list owner before they go out to everybody else. This way, rude or inappropriate messages can be cut out before everybody else gets to them.

Find out more information about mailing lists, check out:
http://www.yahoo.co.uk/Computers_and_Internet/Internet/Mailing_Lists/

This section of Yahoo contains simply thousands of lists for you to join, as well as ways of setting up your own list.

Virus hoaxes

Almost a form of spam, virus hoaxes are incredibly common on the Internet. These hoaxes pray on the gullibility and/or lack of technical knowledge of their unwitting victims. They usually claim that there is a new virus on the loose, which travels via email. The claims usually go on to say that if you receive an email with a certain subject, you should delete it at once or risk having your hard drive shredded. All (yes, all) of these warnings are hoaxes, no matter if they say the information was sent out by Microsoft, IBM, or the Queen. Viruses can be attached to program files that people might send you, but you would have to actually run the program to become infected.

One major ISP even sent out one of these ridiculous warnings a year or so back to all of its customers, and refused to admit that that they had been taken in by a hoax. So, if you've been taken in, don't feel too bad. Even big companies can be ill-informed. If you are worried that someone has sent you a hoax, check out the site: http://ciac.llnl.gov/ciac/CIACHoaxes.html. All shall be explained.

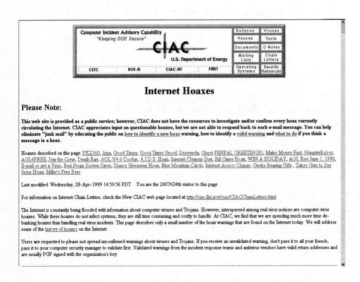

Anonymous Remailers

It's not just spies, terrorists and perverts that want their privacy. There are many acceptable reasons for wanting to keep your identity a secret online. For example, you may wish to make some comments to your boss without him/her knowing who sent them, you may wish to confess to something, without having the whole world know who you are, or you may just want to post pictures of yourself to an 'artistic' Newsgroup. Well, there are many options open to the security conscious among you. The best are anonymous remailers. They are fairly simple in design - you send a mail to the remailer, with a line at the top of the email stating the address of the person you want to contact. The remailer then strips all the information concerning your email address, IP address (your physical address on the Internet - not your email address), ISP and name from the email, and sends the new, cut down version to the final recipient. This way if the recipient tries to trace the sender, he or she would just end up at the remailer, and not at your front door. You are also usually assigned a unique identifying number, so that if the recipient replies, you will actually receive it. Of course, this means that the remailer must hold your real address on file - and if the police wanted to get hold of that information, they probably could. Remailers are usually free, but the classier operations (usually Web based) do charge. Of course, this removes another layer of privacy (they may need credit card numbers, for instance).

Simple in theory but often the opposite in practice, anonymous remailers are the tool of the geeky pros. If you want to learn more about them, then point your browser towards http://www.stack.nl/~galactus/remailers/. This site hasn't been updated for a while, but it's fairly comprehensive, and provides masses of privacy tips, email related and otherwise.

A Recap of email netiquette

Some of these tips will already have been briefly mentioned in this chapter, but it's worth going over them one more time. The quicker you learn these, the quicker people on the Net will actually treat you with some respect. It may seem harsh, but that's the way it goes.

Firstly, never, ever send out unsolicited emails to anybody. If you do, you deserve all of the abuse and flak you'll get as a result of it.

Secondly, you should never send emails written entirely in capital letters. Capital letters are considered to be 'shouting'. However, sending email entirely in lower-case is acceptable.

Thirdly, never send files to somebody without obtaining their permission (this may not be so important with very small files - use common sense).

Finally, never send or forward 'chain mails' or pyramid scams. Simple really isn't it?

5-Newsgroups

Newsgroups (otherwise known as Usenet) are the best way of talking to people whom you know have similar interests to yourself. It's best to think of it as a message board. You email your messages to the board, where other people can pick them up and reply to them if they feel like it. Actually, it's a little more complicated than that. There are many thousands of message boards, all of which communicate with each other and share the same information, so it all acts as though there was only one. It works using email, so it's pretty simple to get involved in.

There are Newsgroups on every topic imaginable. There are thousands of them out there, and they cater for more or less every interest. When you find one that looks as though it would interest you, all you need to do is 'subscribe' to it. This isn't quite as it sounds - you aren't really subscribing to anything as such, so don't worry. It just means that you can use the group if you want to. So, once you're on board, all you need to do is click on any message you want to read. It will then come up on the screen, and you can either reply to it, or ignore it. You can send your reply to either the author of the posting or the Newsgroup itself. Most people post to the Newsgroup so that any other interested parties can read their reply.

It's not just text either, any kind of files can be posted to Newsgroups. Files are encoded, and sent in text form. When somebody sees the file you've posted and wants to view or play it, they just use their Newsgroup software to decode the file. This makes the Newsgroups very popular for people wanting to exchange pictures and sound or video files. If you're a little confused, don't worry. It really is very simple, and in a few minutes you too could be catching up on the latest news and gossip, or downloading fake pictures of posh spice.

Unfortunately, Usenet suffers severely from spam. Spam, as reported in our email chapter, is unsolicited and unwelcome commercial email. The first major spam of Usenet was perpetrated in 1994 by hapless US legal firm Canter and Siegel (Canter now having been disbarred). They were unrepentant in their activities, having sent over the same post to tens of thousands of different Newsgroups - they even threatened to do it again, and CNN reported that they were pioneering entrepreneurs! This was in the days before the media, often slow on the uptake, discovered just how annoying spam could be. These days, spam is prevalent in most Newsgroups. The people that send it are generally considered to be the lowest form of scum on the Internet, but there's little anybody can do about it now.

What you will need

In order to read and post News you will need your News server location, and your login name and password (usually the same ones you use to connect). You will also need a piece of software (see below) and an email account if you wish to post. You usually use your normal email address.

News servers are almost always in the format news.isp.net. For example, Eidosnet users will use news.eidosnet.co.uk, and Freeserve users will use news.freeserve.co.uk.

The Software

Whilst there is plenty of choice when it comes to Newsgroup software, the three best options are Agent, Netscape and Outlook.

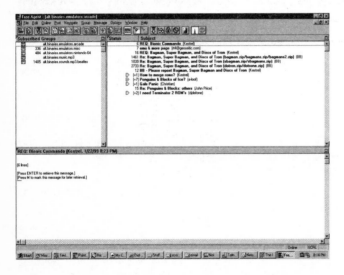

Agent / Free Agent

http://www.forte.com

Forte Agent is considered by the Newsgroup pros to be the best of the best. It has a massive range of options and features. It can do so many things that it'd take you ages to find them all out. This does have the unwanted side effect of making things really cluttered and hard to understand, however. Agent is great if you have a lot of patience, but it has it's problems. For example, pictures cannot be viewed in Agent - it can download and decode them, but they would have to be viewed by a different piece of software. The major advantage it has is that it can decode multi-part files (see later in the chapter) - something that Netscape can't. This makes Agent essential if you want to download really large files - but Netscape can deal with the 99.9% of picture files which are made up of only one post. Agent is not free, but there is a demo version available called Free Agent. It's worth checking out if you think you'll want to take Newsgroups seriously.

Netscape

http://www.netscape.com

Netscape's built in Newsgroup software is pretty good. It decodes and displays picture files on the fly, and sorts threads (see below) out in a very logical way. It's the best choice for casual Newsgroup users or those that really can't be bothered with the hassle of Agent. The big bonus is that it works really well with the Netscape email facilities, and if you can use Netscape mail, you can use the Newsgroup functions too. It is simple, quick, and straightforward.

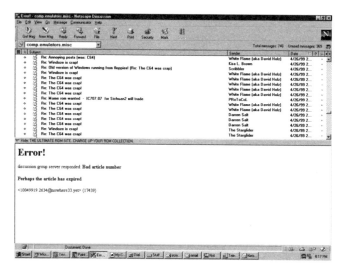

Outlook

http://www.microsoft.com/ie/

Microsoft's mailer also acts as a Newsgroup reader. It works in a very similar way to everyday email, so you can't go far wrong with it. You just enter in your news server address, and away you go.

Subscribing

So, you've got the software. Now how do you use it? Well, that's simple. If you get Agent, just read the Help file. It is a good read and should get you started in no time. Netscape and Outlook are even easier - if you can use email you'll have no problems. You can create new messages, reply and forward in the same way as if dealing with conventional email. If you're in Netscape, just click on the speech bubbles in the bottom right of the Netscape window. If you're in Outlook, simply select 'Newsgroups' from the Tools menu. In Netscape, you can right click on the name of your News server (if you haven't done this, go to the File menu and select 'New Discussion Group Server'), and click 'Subscribe to Discussion Groups' to download the list of groups (be warned, this takes ages). Internet Explorer should prompt you for the necessary details, and then begin the download of Newsgroups. You can then search the Newsgroup titles for keywords, or just scroll down the list and subscribe to any that take your fancy. When you're done, click OK, click the Plus symbol next to the News server name, then click on the Newsgroup name of your choice, and you're away.

The Groups

It's strongly recommended that the first group you visit is alt.test. This provides a safe way of being able to mess around and test things out without annoying the users on the proper groups. You can post to it and read the various messages in it, to try and get the hang of things. That's what it's for. Don't post to a proper group with a message that reads 'just testing'.

The Newsgroup hierarchy may initially seem quite daunting, but it's really pretty simple. All Newsgroup names are made up of at least two parts. Firstly, they have a top level category name. For example, in the case of alt.test, this would be 'alt'. The Alt category is the anarchic part of Usenet, in which thousands of groups reside. Anyone with the knowledge can propose a group for the Alt category, and so there thousands of them available. This is where most of the pornography groups reside, but also a great deal of perfectly 'clean' groups. There's a lot of effort involved in getting a Newsgroup created in any of the other categories, and Alt provides a quick way of doing it without going through the ridiculous process of trying to get people to vote to create a group. If you want to create your own Newsgroup in the alt hierarchy, check out http://www.cis.ohio-state.edu/~barr/alt-creation-guide.html

Here are some of the other main categories:

comp - Computer related talk.

uk - Groups concerning UK issues.

rec - Recreational activities

misc - Enough said.

news - Information about Usenet itself.

If a group has 'binaries' in it's title, then it means that the group is intended for files only. These could be pictures, sounds, movies or any other kind of file.

Do I have access to every group?

Probably not. Some providers such as UKOnline and Eidosnet provide very good access to groups, but unfortunately many don't. This can be due to a few considerations: News servers take up a lot of hard disk space, and some companies are not willing to allocate resources for them. There are also a lot of ISPs that, for moral reasons, won't provide access to groups containing pornography or pirated music/software. These types of ISP will often add non-offensive groups to their lists if you ask nicely. If they refuse, you can change ISPs.

Threads

When someone makes a posting to a Newsgroup, they start a thread. When people reply to that posting, their message is added to the thread.

This makes it easy to read through a discussion. When somebody posts a reply, the subject is automatically prefixed with 'RE:'. This way, the News reader can sort the postings by subject, and then by date. Often threads need to be opened - that is, there will be a plus symbol before the subject of a particular posting. Click the + to expand the thread, and read all of the replies.

Files

A lot of people use the Newsgroups to get files. The most common of these take the form of pornographic pictures, but there are also many other binary groups out there. If you are using Netscape, then viewing pictures is easy. You just click on the posting that contains the file, and the file is decoded and displayed as it downloads. If you want to save it, you click on it with the right mouse button and select 'Save As'. Easy. You can usually (but not always) tell whether a posting contains a file by checking the subject. If it has something.jpg in it, then it will contain an image. Another way of telling is by whether or not the subject contains numbers, in the format [1/1]. This signifies that the file is contained within one posting. If the number were to read [1/3], it would mean that there are two other postings which contain parts of this file. This is because the software used by the person making the posting decided that the file was too large to send in just one mail, and it had to split it up. This rarely happens with pictures, but is common with large files (sounds, movies, software etc.). Netscape can't deal with multi-part files, but Agent automatically seeks out the remaining parts of any file you're trying to download.

Netiquette

You're probably dying to start posting to various Newsgroups, but the best advice is to wait a while first. Spend some time just watching the groups that you are interested in, checking out the new postings every day. It's so easy to make mistakes when it comes to posting to groups that quite a large majority of first-time posters do something pretty stupid on their first attempt. There are some rules that should always be followed if you plan on posting to Newsgroups:

1) Never, ever post 'make money quick' or MLM (Multi Level Marketing) scam-postings to Newsgroups! If you do this, you may be forced from your ISP. The same applies to conventional email, not just Newsgroups. If you do this, you deserve to lose your Internet account. Virgin Internet have taken legal action in the UK against people that have spammed its users.

2) Never write in capitals. This is the equivalent of shouting. When people write entire posts in capitals, they appear as if they have no clue what they are doing.

3) Never respond to an email with 'Me too'. If you agree with a posting, then say why you agree with it - posts made up of just two words are pointless.

4) Don't ask stupid questions. Before you ask, always read through the existing posts in a group to see if somebody else has already asked the same question. If you're too lazy to look through the group for an answer to your question, why should anyone else go to the effort on your behalf? Always look for an FAQ (Frequently Asked Questions) in the group before you post!

5) Resist the temptation to 'flame' (get very upset with). There are racists, perverts and sadly deranged people on the Net, but don't fall into the trap of slagging them off. It's a waste of space, and it just gives the idiots what they want. Many of these people are termed 'trolls'. This means that they post offensive views in order to gain a response from people. Don't give them the satisfaction.

6) Don't cross-post. Cross-posting is where you post to more than one group at once. Even if it seems as though more than one group is related to the subject of the mail, don't do it. Post separate mails to each of the groups if you must, but crossposting is not appreciated.

7) Never post files to groups that don't have 'binaries' in their name. Many people read their News offline (see page 75), and they don't want to have to download binary files, which will increase their time connected to the Internet, and hence cost them money. It'll also get you into awful trouble.

8) Never post virus warnings to Newsgroups. No matter how certain you are that a virus warning is genuine, don't post it. They are very rarely genuine anyway, and you'll just be wasting your time. An exception to this is if somebody has posted an executable file to a Newsgroup, which you have downloaded and found to contain a virus. If this is the case, it's commendable to make a posting to warn people of the risk.

These may seem like common-sense points, but it doesn't stop hundreds of people every day from posting 'get rich quick' scams. Always follow the above guidelines, and you should be OK. But it's still advisable to watch the groups for a little while before you make your first posting.

DejaNews

Once a posting has been sent, it remains on the various News servers for a period of time not usually exceeding a week. After that, the posting will be lost forever - or will it? Well, thankfully, the vast majority of postings made since 1996 have been archived on a Web site called DejaNews (http://www.dejanews.com). Unfortunately, no files are stored (no pictures or whatever), but almost all of the text postings are. You can search the Newsgroups for any information you might need. Searches can be by groups or by dates - it really is a useful research tool.

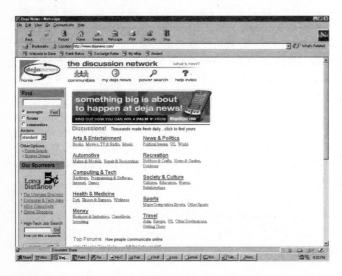

How to Avoid Getting Spam

Sadly, getting spam (or junk email) is an inevitable part of being a part of the Usenet community - or at least it was. Spammers have software which scans the Newsgroups and harvests all of the email addresses contained within the postings. There are ways of stopping it, but they're a little long winded. The best way to stop the spammers is to change your address in your chosen News reader. If you're using Netscape, this means changing the section which reads 'Email Address', in the 'identity' section of the preference screen. Say your email address is bob@boredom.org. You could change it to be bob@numbernine.boredom.org. Then just add to the bottom of any postings that you make that anyone wanting to contact you via email should remove the first part of the domain name from your email address before they try and contact you. Be warned that the software used by these evil spammers is getting very complicated, and it can easily spot email addresses which have just had something like 'nospam' inserted into them, and just remove that part of the address. You'll probably get used to spam mail in the end, and until laws can be passed to have these people prosecuted, it looks like you don't have much choice.

Reading Offline

If you like to read most of the postings in a particular group, you may find it easier to read them offline. What happens here is that your News software will download all of the postings in a group, and allow you to read them once you've disconnected from the Internet. If you want to reply to a posting, you can write out your reply and it will end up in the outbox until you reconnect, whereupon your reply will be sent (either manually or automatically) to the server. This can save a lot of time and money, but it isn't as popular as it used to be. You can use Microsoft's OutLook program to effectively read Newsgroups offline.

Kill Files

Most News readers will give you the option of adding someone to your 'Kill File'. This doesn't involve paying someone to kill an individual, but it does allow you to ignore all postings from a particular individual. The News reader will automatically filter out any postings from someone you don't like, thus saving you a bit of downloading time. Some News readers may use filters instead of a Kill File, which are capable of the same task.

6-Downloading Software

One of the most useful and practical aspects of the Internet is the ability to get hold of free software. This software, usually called 'shareware' is made freely available to anyone who wants it. The term 'shareware' usually refers to software that is provided on a demonstration basis. This means that if you decide you'd like to keep it, then you have to pay a small fee to the programmer. Often shareware is crippled or time-limited, so that you will have no choice but to register it if you like it. Then when you pay, you will be provided with a serial number (which you enter into the software to unlock special functions), or the full version of the software. This kind of shareware is sometimes called Crippleware, for obvious reasons.

Another, less common form of software is 'freeware'. Freeware is, obviously, totally free. Less common still is giftware, where you are asked to send a small present to the programmer - usually beer or something similar.

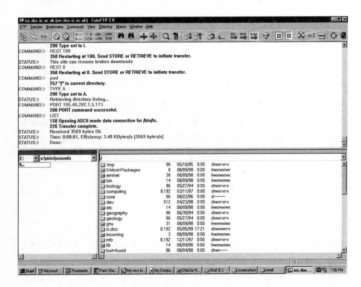

Often you can just use the Web to get hold of software, but there will probably be occasions where you will have to use something called FTP.

What is FTP?

FTP stands for File Transfer Protocol. It works in a very different way to the Web, although most browsers can handle FTP sites if they need to. You'd be advised to get hold of a proper FTP client rather than relying on your browser though, since browsers tend to miss out several of the most important features. For example, FTP software can restart downloads. So if you get disconnected when a download is at 99.5%, you can simply restart the download from the point where you got disconnected, which can save a lot of time.

Basically, when you connect to an FTP server, it's as though you can look around on the remote computer. You can look inside directories, copy files from the server to your own machine, and often upload your own files to the server. In the good old days you had to use text commands to look around - text commands which would be very familiar to UNIX users. These days, most software uses a simple point and click interface.

How do I use it?

Well, despite the fact that downloading direct from the Web is becoming ever more popular, FTP sites are still quite important. Most people take FTP for granted, and simply use their browsers to access FTP sites.

To access a site using your browser, you must type this into the address field: ftp://<sitename>. This tells the browser that it's an FTP site, so that it knows how to communicate with it. As an example, try ftp://src.doc.ic.ac.uk. This is the UK Sunsite server. It contains an insane amount of freely distributable software for PC, Mac, UNIX and Amiga computers. When it's done, you should see a listing of the contents of the initial directory. Unfortunately, Sunsite is so huge that you'd be unlikely to find what you're looking for without knowing exactly where it resides. However, it could be useful for you to have a look around and get the feel for using it. If you'd like to get a better idea of the software available on the site, then you can visit the Web site - which is the same address, but prefixed with http:// instead of ftp://.

The best method, however, is to use a proper client. Browsers are all very well, but they don't have the 'resume' function, and they work in a slightly different way to normal clients. Suffice to say that many system administrators would prefer you used a proper client - it makes their logs more tidy.

There are many different FTP clients out there, but one of the best for the PC is CuteFTP (http://www.cuteftp.com). It's shareware, and as such is limited to a 30 day trial until you register. However, it's got a lot of functions and is easy to use. Setting up a connection is simple, and it also allows you to keep trying busy sites until you can get in. This is handy for sites which have restrictions on the amount of people that can log in at once. CuteFTP can retry the connection every 30 seconds whilst you get on and do something else. However, make sure that you don't 'hammer' the site - that is, set it to retry the connection every second - this can really slow down a server and could get you permanently banned from using it!

CuteFTP has simple upload and download functions. All you need to do is drag and drop files to transfer them. You will hardly ever have occasion to type any commands, since they're all available in menu items and icons. This is true of all of the main FTP programs for PCs and Macs. If, however, you decide to connect using a text based connection then see later on in the chapter.

What's this about being anonymous?

Unless you have an account on an FTP server, you will login as 'anonymous'. The password usually has to be your email address. If you're using a browser, then it'll deal with this for you transparently. Remember though that you aren't actually anonymous, you can still be traced back to your ISP, and even to your username! Remember this when using FTP sites, and always be responsible.

Uploading your web site

The most likely reason that you will have use an FTP server is to update your Web site. Your ISP will most likely give you your own FTP account, which you log into using your normal login name and password. It should automatically dump you into the correct directory. All you need to do then is to upload the necessary files. You can also delete files, as long as they belong to you.

Text connections

In the old days, you had to use text commands to negotiate FTP sites - and you still can if you like. It's very easy, but PC based clients such as CuteFTP make the task a bit quicker. If you can only connect to the Internet using a text based connection, or you wish to connect using a UNIX account, then this example should help you to understand how to connect and guide you through the first steps.

The example is spaced out to make it a bit clearer, and explanations are provided as to what is going on throughout. Anything in italics is what was typed - the rest is what was output by the FTP server. It isn't usually in italics, this is just for the sake of making things clearer.

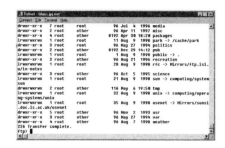

In this example, we know that a file named goober.avi exists on a server named 'ftp.somewhere.net'. That's all we know, and we have to find and download this file.

--example begins--

[bob:/usr/home/neon] *ftp ftp.somewhere.net* [**connects to the server**]
Connected to ftp.somewhere.net.
220-****** Welcome to the somewhere.net archives ******
220-Anonymous access is allowed through a login of 'anonymous'.
220-You must send your *complete* email address as the password.
220-
220 ftp.somewhere.net FTP server (Version wu-2.4(1) Fri Jan 17 12:05:30 MST 1997) ready.

Name : *anonymous* [**this is the login name - you usually enter 'anonymous'**]

331 Guest login ok, send your complete e-mail address as password.

Password: *my@mail.com* [**with an anonymous login, you enter your email address as the password**]

230 Guest login ok, access restrictions apply.
Remote system type is UNIX.
Using binary mode to transfer files.

ftp> *ls* [**get an initial directory listing - see what directories are available**]
200 PORT command successful.

150 Opening ASCII mode data connection for /bin/ls.
total 14
drwxr-xr-x root wheel 512 Dec 15 1997 bin
drwxr-xr-x root wheel 512 Dec 15 1997 etc
drwx-x-x root wheel 512 Dec 15 1997 hidden
drwx—- root wheel 512 Sep 25 1997 incoming
drwxr-xr-x root wheel 512 Feb 16 14:07 pub
drwxr-xr-x root wheel 512 Dec 15 1997 shlib
drwxrwxrwx root wheel 512 Nov 6 10:55 upload

[The above directory listing may look hard to understand, but it's quite easy. The first part shows permissions and suchlike, and isn't really important. The fourth part is though - it shows the file size. Seeing as all of the things listed here are directories and not files, they are all displayed as being 512 bytes in size. Remember that bytes are used and not kilobytes. Divide the number given by 1000 to get the size in kilobytes.]

ftp> *cd pub* **[enter the directory named 'pub' - pub is usually where everything public is stored]**
250 CWD command successful.

ftp> *ls* **[get a listing of the files and directories in the 'pub' folder]**
200 PORT command successful.

150 Opening ASCII mode data connection for /bin/ls.
total 1258
-rw-r-r- 1 root   wheel   173 Feb 16 14:06 moop.bat
drwxr-xr-x 2 112   user   512 Dec 15 1997 vz
-rwxr-xr-x 1 root   wheel   630116 Oct 30 1997 goober.avi
drwxr-xr-x 2 root   wheel   512 Dec 15 1997 modem-stats
drwxr-xr-x 2 granite   user   512 Dec 15 1997 quake
drwxr-xr-x 2 root   wheel   512 Dec 15 1997 soxmas
226 Transfer complete.

ftp> *get goober.avi* **[download goober.avi - a video file]**
local: goober.avi remote: goober.avi

200 PORT command successful.
150 Opening BINARY mode data connection for goober.avi (630116 bytes).
226 Transfer complete.

--example ends--

That was typical of any normal FTP session. There may be some changes depending on
the server being used, but the commands used are always the same. Here is a summary
of all the main functions used during FTP.

ls	-	List the files in a directory.
cd <directory>	-	'Change Directory'. 'cd ..' will move back a directory.
get <filename>	-	Download a file.
put <filename>	-	Upload a file.
bin	-	Set binary downloads. See below.
asc	-	Ascii mode downloads.

Binary or Ascii?

Most files (programs, pictures and sounds etc) are binary files. However, text and HTML
files are ascii files. Everything will need to be transferred over the Internet in the right
mode, otherwise your computer won't know how to deal with them. So, if you're trying
to download a text file using FTP, it might be an idea to type 'asc' and then return
beforehand. This just ensures that the server knows how to send the file to you. Similarly,
if it's a binary file, you could type 'bin'. This is usually automatic, but things do go wrong
sometimes.

If you've accidentally downloaded a binary file in ascii mode (this does happen sometimes),
then all is not lost. You need to find a program called 'uncook', which will change the
file back into binary. It doesn't have a homepage, but you'll be able to find it somewhere
by using AltaVista (http://www.altavista.com). Uncook comes as a MS DOS or Windows
program. If using the DOS version the command is 'uncook <brokenfile> <newfile>'. Newfile
is the name of the fixed file, since uncook doesn't overwrite the original file.

Downloading via the Web

The Web has recently become the most popular method of downloading files, and these
days there are very few circumstances in which FTP connections have any advantage over

downloading via the Web.

Download.com (http://www.download.comand) and Shareware.com (http://www.shareware.com) provide reasonably good directories of software which can be searched through (you can even use them to find some decent FTP clients), and with the help of software such as GoZilla! and GetRight, you can even resume interrupted downloads.

Gozilla (http://www.gozilla.com) is basically free, though it does have a small banner at the top of the program window which updates itself with advertising (this is called the sponsored version). You can pay to get the full version with no advertising. GoZilla also has several other useful features. It can be used to 'leech' from a Web site - so if a page has several dozen files you'd like to download, you can tell GoZilla to download them each in turn, whereas otherwise you'd have to manually download one file as one finishes. GoZilla can do it all for you without supervision. GetRight (http://www.getright.com) is another piece of software with similar features. Without one of these programs, you'd have an awful job of trying to download large programs over the Web.

WinZip

Almost all software that you download will be in ZIP form. This means that 'WinZip' or another zip program has compressed it. Zip is the most popular way of compressing and decompressing files for transmission over the Internet. WinZip is shareware, and essential for anyone wanting to download software. You can get it from http://www.winzip.com. Once WinZip is installed, it will automatically ensure that Windows knows what to do when you double click a Zip file. It'll open it up, and then all you need to do is select 'extract' from the 'Actions' menu. Make sure you haven't got just one of the files in the archive selected when you extract though, otherwise only that file will be extracted. It's a simple program, but you'll certainly need it.

7-Chat

If you want to talk to somebody in the States, would you rather phone them up and spend a packet, or do it online whilst surfing the Web, for no extra charge? No competition.

There are lots of places to meet people online, and there are also lots of places packed full of sleazy old men and undesirables. To avoid this, you have to visit small talkers or topic-specific chat areas. One of the less sleazy ways to chat online is to visit a small Talker.

Talkers are like mini-communities, in that you'll soon get to know most of the other regulars. Anybody can make friends this way, it's not any sort of exclusive club. You don't even have to know a thing about computers to get on - a lot of the users are university students who have little or no computer knowledge, having been introduced to it by friends. There are also a number of more mature users.

There is also an entirely different form of Internet chat, known as IRC (Internet Relay Chat). IRC is a bit of a different monster, but allows for more specific types of chat.

Web-based chat is also popular in it's own peculiar way, but compared to the alternatives it is fairly slow and cumbersome.

ICQ is a totally different thing again, allowing for posting of files back and forth, leaving messages and finding people with similar interests.

What is it all about?
A lot of people are negative towards Internet chat - they think it's a bit of a sad activity. The fact is, the majority of people that use the Internet to talk to others are perfectly normal people, and it's possible to make some really good friends. Some people even find husbands and wives online!

People unable to get out and meet people very often can find great comfort in the Internet. When you log onto a talker, nobody knows anything about your appearance, so talk is without all the issues that labelling people can have. You only need tell people things about yourself if you want to.

Meeting Internet friends in real life is a very common activity - either as part of a large group (talkers often have large meets), or as a one to one meeting down the pub. It could turn out that you end up speaking to your Internet friends in real life more than you do online!

Before you start chatting, it's probably best to try and work out what kind of chat you're looking for. If you just want to meet various different people, all with different interests, then you'd probably want to try talkers at first. If you want to discuss something in particular - for example, your favourite band or computer game, then IRC is the best way forwards. Both are covered in this chapter.

IRC

IRC is famous and notorious in equal measures. It is famous for being the world's most popular chat format - except possibly AOL chat - and infamous for being the lair of pirates of virtually every description. Entire films, CDs, and full-versions of computer software are all available on IRC to those who have the technology or the patience. And that's not to mention the more unpleasant IRC channels which you will want to avoid. For this reason, IRC is not really suitable for children. But, if you're responsible, IRC can be a great discussion medium. It can also keep you updated with all of the latest news on a whole variety of software. Remember that a lot of it is rubbish though, IRC is the world's biggest gossip medium! Also, don't expect to be treated gently in most channels. Many people on IRC are sad nerds that don't have much tolerance for newbies.

The Networks

There are a number of different IRC networks. Each is completely unconnected, and contains totally different channels. The main two, and the only two you'll probably ever need, are UnderNet and EFnet. Dalnet is becoming more popular, but most networks are more or less identical in terms of usage and syntax anyway.

The Channels

To talk on IRC once connected to a server, you have to join a channel. A channel is like a separate room, where people with similar interests can gather. Channel names are always prefixed with a # symbol. To create your own channel, you just need to join a channel that doesn't exist - and you will have created it! It'll go away again once there's nobody left on it.

The Software

PC users will want to use a piece of software called mIRC, available at http://www.mirc.co.uk. Mac users should use Ircle (http://www.xs4all.nl/~ircle/) or Homer.

Setting Up

Setting yourself up for an IRC section is incredibly easy. Once you've installed the program of your choice, you simple load it up and fill in a brief preferences page. This usually includes putting in a nickname (the name you'll be known by online) and your email address (you should consider using a false address though in the interests of safety) - IRC has its share of lunatics. When it comes to connecting to an IRC server, your software will contain a list of reasonably current servers that you can choose from. It's best to pick one in England for speed considerations. If your chosen software doesn't include any servers, then here are just a few of the many servers available:

EFnet
efnet.demon.co.uk
efnet.sto.telia.se
irc-2.netcom.com

UnderNet
london.uk.eu.undernet.org
chicago.il.us.undernet.org
okc.ok.us.undernet.org

Unfortunately, it's quite common for something to go wrong during the connection process. This can be because the server is down or full. It could also have been the victim of a netsplit. This means that the server you have connected with has become disconnected from the other servers in the network. If this happens just pick another server and try again.

Once you connect, you will probably be shown the MOTD (Message of the Day), and then dumped unceremoniously into the deep end. At first, you can't talk to anyone because you aren't in a room (or 'channel'). To list all of the channels, type /list (and be prepared for a considerable wait). All commands used in IRC have to be prefixed with a forward slash. Anything not prefixed with a forward slash will be considered something you intend to broadcast to the rest of the channel. When you find a channel you want to join, double click on it to enter the discussion. If you already know the name of the channel you want to join you do not need to do the listing. You can just type '/join #channelname'. Once you've joined a group, your software will show you a listing of all the people on that group, and the discussion they are having. You're probably better off to just watch people talking for a bit before you say anything. Like Newsgroups, IRC is a great way of making a complete idiot out of yourself. There are a number of things which you should know before you actually say anything on IRC - most of which will be familiar from the Newsgroups chapter.

1)   Never talk in caps.
2)   Never lose your temper with anyone.
3)   Don't ask stupid questions.
4)   Don't keep repeating yourself

As usual, these are common sense points. If you annoy anyone on IRC, you can be kicked off (and even banned) from a channel. Just be sensible and you should be fine.

When you feel confident enough to join in the discussion, you just need to type something into the provided field and press enter. Let's say you log on as 'Newbie', and typed 'Hello!', people would see this:

Newbie: Hello!

Pretty easy. If you want to 'emote' something, you need to type /me before it. For example, if you typed '/me yawns', everyone would see:

Newbie yawns

There will probably be occasions when you want to send a private message to someone. The simplest way to do this is to use the msg command. Let's imagine you wanted to say hi to Bob. You could type '/msg bob Hi!'. Bob would then get the private message. With most IRC clients (including mIRC), upon receiving a msg from somebody, you should open a special window. In this window, you can chat privately to the person in question without having to type /msg before it each time.

On the other hand, you could use DCC chat. DCC chat bypasses the IRC network, so that messages you send to each other will go straight to each other's machines. Which brings us to...

DCC

DCC is a method of sending files over IRC. You can send a file to somebody without it going through the IRC network.

To offer a file to somebody over IRC you should use the DCC Send option in your chosen piece of software. For receiving you just need to click 'Accept' when someone offers you a file. However, never download a file without knowing what it is - it could be virus infected. For the same reason, never set your IRC client to automatically receive files.

If your client doesn't have an automatic send/receive function, you have to use these commands:

/dcc send <name> <file, ie: c:\file.doc>
/dcc receive <person who is offering you the file>

With these basics you should have no problems in getting the hang of IRC. If you do have any problems which aren't covered here, then join a group such as #newbies. There's sure to be someone who can help you, but be patient.

Talkers

The best introduction to online chat would be to use a talker. IRC can be scary, and it's easy to make mistakes, for which you will be mercilessly mocked and abused. Talkers are generally more laid back and an awful lot more friendly. They're also incredibly easy to use. Many talker users are fairly computer illiterate, as no technical knowledge is required to use them. Telnet is the software that you use for Talkers.

So what's Telnet?

Telnet is a nice, though simplistic piece of software which allows you to connect to another computer and use it as though you were sitting in front of it - though only in a text-based form. You have to type commands, and the mouse isn't used at all. For this reason, people who want to connect to machines that run UNIX based operating systems (which are traditionally accessed by typing commands anyway) often use Telnet. Using Telnet you could, say, connect to a work machine from home, and do many of the tasks that you could do by being at that machine, including dealing with email and Web-site updating. Alternatively you could just use it talk to people.

The first steps

Firstly, get Telnet loaded. If you have a PC, you should go to the 'Start' menu, and click on 'Run'. Type 'Telnet' into the field and press enter. Note that this only loads Windows Telnet - a pretty poor effort by anyone's standards, with a few problems.

If you intend on using Talkers frequently, you'd better get a copy of Gmud, from http://aria.wolfpaw.net/~baria/gmud.html (which isn't the official site - that doesn't appear to exist anymore), or, if you don't mind spending ages setting it up, MushClient (http://www.gammon.com.au/mushclient/). Once you have Windows Telnet up and running, go to the Terminal Menu, and select 'Preferences'. If 'Local Echo' isn't ticked, tick it. Otherwise you won't be able to see what you're typing.

On a Mac, you'll need to get NCSA Telnet which you can find on one of many Mac shareware sites. NCSA Telnet is probably the best Telnet client on any platform - easy to use and to work with.

Telnet sites always use not only an Internet address, but also a four-letter port number. This is because each server on the Internet has a number of 'slots', which can each be running different programs. For example, one of the slots could be occupied by a talker, one could be occupied by a Web server, and one could be running an FTP server. When you connect to the machine, you need to let it know which slot you want to connect to - so you need to supply a port number. Web and FTP servers have default ports to occupy, talkers do not.

So assuming that you have a Telnet client loaded, it's pretty easy from here onwards. Select the 'Connect to remote system' menu item (or equivalent), and type 'zeta.aquilae.org' in the server field. In the field marked 'Port', type 3456. If there is no port field, try typing 'zeta.aquilae.org 3456' or 'zeta.aquilae.org:3456' into the main field - one of those should work! All Telnet clients work differently, but the documentation should tell you which method to use.

Press enter, and you could be presented with a title screen. Zeta Aquilae is an English talker which was set up (in it's original form) four years ago. It has a loyal band of friendly 'locals', and you're pretty much guaranteed a friendly reception. You can also be sure that the people you're talking to really are who they claim to be - most of them are involved in 'meets' in real life. No hairy-handed old perverts on Zeta (except the ones who freely admit to it).

Zeta is a good introduction to talkers because it doesn't throw you in at the deep end, and you don't get confronted by lowlife before you even know how to use it. It also works in the same way as all of the other popular talkers, so it's a nice method of getting used to the commands in a friendly environment.

Well, you probably want to log on at this point. You have to enter a login name - this could be anything really, but remember that your login name is how people will know you once online. So, no swear words, nothing rude, and generally not your real name (but that's up to you). Common choices are words or names that are in some way significant - nicknames, for example. Once you've chosen a name, type it in and then press enter. Hopefully, if there are any members of staff (people who 'police' the talker, as well as look after new users) online, then you'll be given all of the introductory information. If there are no staff online, you're stuck - and you'll have to try again later. Assuming you made it on OK, follow all of the instructions to the letter, and soon you'll find yourself logged in. Eventually, you should see something like this (note that all of the names are made up):

There are three other people here ...
Bob is bored
Doughboy
Spoon
->

Of course, exactly what that says will depend upon who is currently logged on. Now, we can see that in this example, Bob has some words after his name - this is called a title, and you don't need to worry about that yet. First off, you might want to say hello to everybody, by typing 'say Hi Everyone!'. If you typed that (and assuming you logged on with the username Newbie), everyone in the room would see:

Newbie exclaims 'Hi everyone!'

If nobody answers, don't worry too much. They're probably 'idle'. Some sad spods stay logged in all day even though they aren't actually paying attention.

If 'Spoon' replied and you wanted to talk to him privately, you'd use the 'tell' command. For example, you might type 'tell spoon Why are you a spoon?'.

Here are some of the first commands you may need:

who	-	Gives a listing of all people currently online. This will list their user names.
lsu	-	Lists all staff members currently online, along with their staff position.
say	-	'Say' something which will be seen by the whole room. Syntax is 'say <whatever>'.
tell	-	Send a private message to a user. Syntax is 'tell <person's name> <whatever>'
x	-	See somebody's profile. Syntax is 'x <person's name>.

It's important to remember that a lot of people will have words before their names. These are called prefixes, and they don't count as a part of the person's name - you don't include them when talking to or about them.

You'd be advised to talk to an administrator to begin with, because they'll know how to help you out the best. They'll also be able to make you a resident - that is, make your login name permanent and give you a password, so that you can always log on, even when no staff are online.

So, to begin with, type 'lsu', and pick one of the names - preferably an administrator, but it doesn't really matter. Then type something like 'tell <name> hello, I'm a newbie, can you give me a hand?'. Of course, exactly what you say is up to you. From here, you should find it very simple. There are many hundreds of different commands and command combinations to learn, but you pick them up slowly over a period of time.

It is important to remember that although it may seem daunting and hard to get to grips with at first, it's actually very simple. A great deal of the people using it have little or no computer skills, so it can't be that difficult! If you get stuck at any point, and there's nobody to help you, type 'help'. If there's a command that you don't fully understand, try 'help <command>'.

If you decide that Zeta isn't big enough for you, there are a few large talkers out there. The biggest in the UK is Surfers. Surfers is large, impersonal, and full of sleaze, but it has a large user base. You can find surfers at http://www.surfers.co.uk.

Web Chat
Web chat has been around since around 1996, but to begin with it was terribly basic and not instant like Telnet or IRC. Recent sites such as Lycos Chat (http://chat.lycos.com) offer half-decent Java programs that you use to access them. They have specific chat areas too, like IRC. However, some of the servers on Lycos chat seem to fill up quite easily, which is a shame. It's still worth trying though, if only for the ease of use. Full instructions are provided to anyone wanting to register and try it out. The only bad point is that Lycos Chat & Yahoo Chat are situated in the US and Canada.

Most of the best chat sites (and a lot of really awful ones) can be found on Yahoo! UK (http://www.yahoo.co.uk/Computers_and_Internet/Internet/World_Wide_Web/Chat/).

Some, such as Yahoo chat are fairly similar to the older style Telnet talkers, but with graphic user interfaces instead of being fully text based. However, they still seem to attract a vastly different person. To some, Web chat can be a little impersonal, although regulars often do meet in certain chat areas. Web chat is also more prone to flirting, talking dirty, and within this context, men pretending to be women (don't even ask why!).

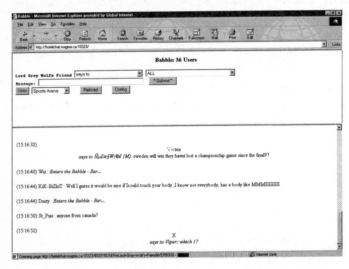

You should ensure that you have a fairly powerful computer if you want to use decent Java based talkers. This doesn't mean you need the latest hardware, but a P166 with 32 Megabytes of RAM is a reasonable minimum. You can use them on lower systems, but be prepared for a pretty slow ride!

Once you get started, you'll soon see other people's conversations going on. Usually, typing something into the field and pressing enter is enough to enter your contribution to the proceedings, but this varies. Almost all chat sites on the web have a page telling you how to get the most out of them.

Yahoo chat offers several buttons. For example, if you click on the name of somebody you wish to talk to and then press 'PM' (Personal Message), you'll be able to talk to that person privately. Most decent chat programs also have an 'Ignore' button. This allows you to ignore selected users so you receive no more messages from them, and you also won't be able to see what they say in public. Strange people will quite often confront you, so it's nice to be able to ignore them. Recently Yahoo launched their UK chat program, so you no longer have to talk to 13 year old American geeks. You can now talk to 13 year old English geeks. Great, then.

You may well find that many of your favourite sites have Web chat added to them, and they may or may not be very popular. It might be good to talk to other visitors to similar sites. Of course, many adult sites provide the opportunity to have live chats with models, but we probably shouldn't go there.

Some TV stations, most notably BBC1, BBC2 and Channel 4, allow viewers to get logged on and talk to their favourite celebs. For more information about these live chats, check out http://www.bbc.co.uk or http://www.channel4.com.

ICQ

ICQ (I Seek You - it's a very poor attempt at a pun) has really taken off in a big way in recent years. It allows you to not only chat to people, but also to keep track of when your friends are on the Internet - as long as they have ICQ installed.

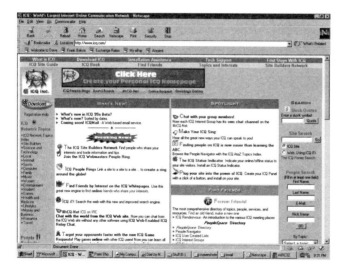

When you install ICQ (available at http://www.icq.com/), it starts up whenever your computer is turned on. Then, whenever you connect to the Internet, it contacts the ICQ server to let it know you're online. It also checks to see how many (if any) of the people on your friends lists are online. If they are, you can send them a chat request, or just send them a quick message. It's not only your friends you can contact either - you can make yourself open to random chat requests. ICQ can automatically select somebody at random for you to chat to, which is an interesting way of meeting people.

ICQ is a very useful piece of software - especially if you want to know when your friends and/or colleagues are online! You certainly won't find any other online chat community with as many users as ICQ.

ICQ is available on PC and Mac systems. A Java port is available, which works on Linux and may allow you to run ICQ on other operating systems such as AmigaOS - though that's largely wishful thinking.

8-Online Gaming

If you know anything about computer games, then you'll have heard of classics such as Unreal, Quake and Half-Life. They are three of the most popular games to have been released in the last ten years, and all three have online functionality. This means that you can connect to special game servers on the Internet, and kill and maim your family, friends and complete strangers. It's a great way of relieving stress, as well as settling old scores!

The real problem with online gaming is that of speed. In recent years, clever programming techniques have managed to overcome a lot of the problems associated with speed, but at the end of the day, there's only so much you can do. Until a minimum of true 56k access methods (that's 56k send and receive, unlike current 56k modems) are invented, you'll have to expect slow connections every now and again. In the case of 3D games, this means that you may get the occasional bit of weird jerkiness, or everything may freeze for a second or two. It is fairly uncommon, and in general it doesn't affect things too much.

Although 3D shooters are by far the most popular online games, there are also Real Time Strategy games that you can play, as well as online adventures. You can even play text-based adventure games (called MUDs or MUCKs), the same ones people played in the eighties. In ten years we've come from text adventures to true 3D shoot 'em ups. Now all we need are some modems that can cope with the amount of data they have to deal with!

Quake III

The long awaited third game arrived in 1999, and improved immensely on the graphical capabilities of the engine. Photo-realism is one of the terms bounded about to describe Quake III, and whilst it's inaccurate, it isn't far from the truth. It really is amazing. The gameplay (running about grabbing supplies and killing everyone) is more or less the same, but it's now a purely multiplayer affair, with no mission structure. If you are playing on your own you

can play against 'bots' though, computer controlled players that come in useful if you are offline. However, as long as you can connect to the Internet, you'll find thousands of like-minded people willing to frag (kill) you all night long.

Tips

1 Don't stay still - ever! If you're shooting at someone, don't stand still and do it - at least use the < and > keys to move left and right whilst doing it. Ideally you should be jumping around a lot also.
2 Rocket jump to higher levels. Run towards the ledge you want to reach, aim at the floor, and fire a rocket. You'll find yourself propelled up into the air! Mind you, you'll probably just frag yourself the first couple of tries.
3 Learn where all of the best weapons are stored in the level.
4 Good players don't camp! Camping is another word for hanging around in one place (usually a nice vantage point where you can see the enemy, but they can't see you). You might get lots of kills, but it won't be through skill.
5 The Quake games are frequently played as team games - so if you're assigned a colour when you connect, make sure you don't spend all of your time blowing the hell out of your own side!

Unreal Tournement

The original Unreal didn't really go down hugely well, at least when it came to Internet play. It was always an amazing game, but it lacked that special spark needed to excite the Interest of the massive numbers of Quake freaks. Then Unreal Tournament was released, and the tables began to turn. There are now plenty that say Unreal Tournament is better than Quake III. For a start, there is a wider range of scenarios and you can kill your opponents in many more different ways than you can in Quake III. Whatever anybody says, if you need to let off some steam, there is nothing as satisfying as a decapitation in Unreal Tournament!

Tribes

Another fantastic online game, Tribes offers you the opportunity to become a jetpack wearing space marine. Jetting over beautiful landscapes, it's your job to fulfil whatever orders are given to you. You can fly in formation with other team members or you can set out on your own to sneak past the enemy. The game offers some truly incredible sights and brilliant action, and has become insanely popular in the States. Some people say that the game is a little quiet – there can be periods where you don't run into any enemies for some time – but it's certainly worth a try, especially if you find Quake and it's contemporaries slightly too frantic for your taste.

Half-Life

Half-Life is generally considered to be the best single player 3D shooter in the world - and with very good reason. Whilst many people are still Quake die-hards, Half-Life offers excellent multiplayer action also. You can use the built-in multiplayer server-finder or you can use the services of Wireplay (explained later). If you use Half-Life online you should really update it on a

regular basis, whenever the patches are released on the official site (http://www.sierra.com). If you are unable to load an Internet game at any time it is usually because your version of the game is now out of date. Loading the latest patch will sort you out. They also often clear up some pretty annoying bugs or problems with previous versions.

Half-Life is popular for many reasons. It has an absolutely brilliant selection of weapons, fantastic levels, and it's amazing plot in the one player game. There are some great Websites for the game, check out: http://www.halflife.org/, http://www.planethalflife.com, http://www.halflife.net/models

Tips

Use the weapons wisely. If you think you can get away with it, use the normal Glock Pistol on enemies - but always aim for the head! The sniper pistol, which looks like something out of the Wild-West, is a particularly deadly weapon when aimed at the head. Remember also to use the shotgun at close range. Clicking the right mouse button blasts off two rounds at once, which is absolutely deadly.

Use the Gauss gun to propel yourself up into the air - like the rocket jump in Quake. Hold down the right mouse button to build up a fairly large supply of energy, then let it go. Don't hold it down for too long though, or you could find yourself thirty feet up in the air - and landing again could be the end of you!

Go for the rocket launcher every time. It's a classic weapon, and once you've mastered it, you can really make the guts fly. Firing a rocket into three or four guys all trying to kill each other with pistols is extremely satisfying. But make sure you click the right mouse button to turn off the bizarre targeting system.

Use the crossbow to shoot people from afar. It's a fantastic way of picking people off. Rockets are good too, but they travel slowly and a rocket can be seen coming from miles away. If you find a good high vantage point, then the crossbow is often the weapon of choice. They won't even know what hit them.

Make your own Spray Paint image! You can spray your own two-colour image onto any surface, and some people have really impressive images. Try to use the gauss gun to propel yourself up a wall and then spray the image into a really prominent position - let them know who's kicking their butt!

Wireplay

Wireplay is a great place to play games on the Internet. Not only does it offer you the chance to play over 140 games (and growing) but it also offers you an incredibly strong community catering for every type of gamer. Whether you like Backgammon or something a bit more upbeat such as Quake 3 there are other gamers of all skill levels who you can play with and chat to.

Wireplay is a matchmaking service that currently enables you to meet and play PC games against thousands of other gamers online. Wireplay itself is not a game, but a small piece of software that can be easily downloaded from Gameplay at http://www.gameplay.com/wireplay. The software is easy to use, just follow the instructions to download and install it. Wireplay is a free service, you just pay your regular online phonebill.

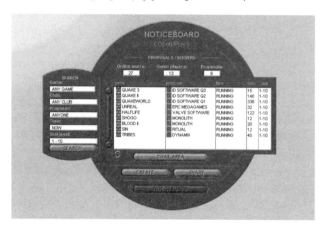

How do I connect to Wireplay ?

You can either use your own ISP (Internet Service Provider) or the dialer that is installed with the Wireplay software. The Powerplay Arena needs you to connect through Wireplay however. The Wireplay dialer is automatically installed with Wireplay software and it offers you the option to connect directly to the Wireplay service for better performance, rather than going via your ISP. The Wireplay dialler charges for calls at a local rate (like most ISP's), the same as making a phone call, there are no extra fees. The Gameplay dialler will automatically tell your modem what number to call and will dial the Wireplay servers when you want to connect – it's that simple. Better performance is expected through the Wireplay dialler as the Wireplay network has been especially configured for Internet gaming traffic.

Once downloaded, Wireplay will scan your hard drive to find any compatible games. If you know you have a compatible title but it doesn't detect it, you can easily add it manually.

Using Wireplay

Wireplay support over 140 games. Most of these games are retail CD games, which means that you have to have the game you want to play installed in your machine. The Wireplay website at offers a selection of free games that can be downloaded and installed fairly quickly. These free games include Air Attack, (a World War 2 Air Combat game that places you in an arena with hundreds of other pilots), and the incredibly popular MUD2, (a text based adventure game).

All this may sound like a fairly unsociable activity, playing against faceless opponents you never see at the other end of the telephone line. That in fact, couldn't be further from the truth. The Wireplay software contains a whole range of functionality that allows you to meet up with other gamers, chat to them either in real-time or through the message boards. You will find various groups in the Wireplay community, with their own chat rooms and message boards, covering a whole host of games.

Browsing through the various game information pages in the Wireplay software (accessed by clicking on the 'info' button) you will find out about all the clubs, clans and leagues that have set themselves up. Clubs hold regular tournaments for all types of games and you can even win some cool prizes. If you start to get serious about your gaming you can join a clan, and play in leagues.

Because of the massive communities that develop around online games, Wireplay appoints a number of well-respected members of the community to assist in the running of the many different communities and the orientation of new players. These are split into 3 categories:

Club Captains/League Masters

These are responsible for running clubs and leagues for specific games. They hold weekly competitions that are open to everyone, whether new to online gaming or old hands. They also produce websites dedicated to their club or league with loads of useful help and are kept up to date with the latest results and rankings. Club Captains are there to help new players and to help you find people of the same skill level.

Community Liaisons

All Community Liaisons were previously Club Captains so they have a lot of experience in running communities. Their job is to liaise between the Club Captains/League Masters and Wireplay staff, to ensure the clubs are running smoothly and the company is meeting the needs of the gamers. The Wireplay software has information about Community Liaisons in the Help section

Gamepros

These are gamers dedicated to helping new players to understand how things operate and how to get their games working on the service. You will find them online every night in the Gamepro chat room if you require any assistance. To access the Gamepro chat room press the 'Gamepro' button displayed in the software.

EidosNet

http://www.eidosnet.co.uk

We have already mentioned Eidosnet in this book, but that was for it's position as an ISP. However, Eidosnet is more than just an ISP. It's an ISP aimed at gamers. It provides not only fully-fledged Internet access, but also a special server called MPlayer which allows you to play a whole host of games including all multiplayer Eidos games online. This is great, because you are guaranteed a decent connection to the server. Usually when you connect to a server on the Internet you could be risking a slow connection. This depends on the amount of computers between you and the server - with Eidosnet, you don't get the same speed problems.

9-MP3

Mpeg 3, or MP3 as it's become known, is the world's premier storage format for large sound files. Using MP3, entire music tracks can be stored in full CD-Quality stereo in as little as one megabyte per minute of sound. This has opened up entirely new ways of transferring audio, and has become very popular on the Internet. It has made it very easy to encode tracks direct from CD. The record industry views this as a major problem because of the obvious piracy factors. More information can be found from the RIAA (Recording Industry Association Of America), at http://www.riaa.com. Although figures show that MP3 would appear not to have any tangible effect on record sales, those same figures can say anything if you misinterpret them badly enough - therefore, many respected musical acts have voiced 'their' disgust at the use of the format as a piracy medium.

It's not all doom, gloom and piracy, however. Some groups have been clever enough to embrace the MP3 format, including major acts such as the Beastie Boys. They have included several special MP3 files on their Web site (http://www.beastieboys.com), which are unavailable anywhere else. Sadly, not many people seem to be following their lead (with the exception of David Bowie).

What do I need to play MP3s?

You'll need a player. There are loads available, but the best one for PC users is Winamp - a tried and tested Windows program that is fast, and stable. You can get it from http://www.winamp.com. It used to be shareware, but it's been completely free since it was snapped up by AOL. Winamp can play MP3 files on most systems above a P100, and it flies on any modern computer. You'll also need a sound card in your computer (they are almost always provided as standard). The better the card, the better the sound will be. The same with the speakers. If you're a Macintosh owner, check out http://www.mp3.com and see what software is available for your machine - for a long time the Mac was well behind the PC for MP3 software, but it's gradually beginning to appear.

Why all the excitement about MP3?

Well, using MP3, you might even be able to fit your entire CD collection on one CD-ROM. You wouldn't be able to listen to that CD in the car (not at the moment, anyway), but it would be of great advantage to anyone who has stacks of CDs piled up alongside their computer. There are also a few different personal MP3 players available now which will allow you to stick your favourite tracks onto a built-in hard drive or writable CD-ROM so that you can play them on the move. Despite the music industry's attempts to block these devices, they're in the shops now.

There's also quite a large supply of bootleg CDs that have been transferred to MP3 format. These are mostly Oasis and Beatles rehearsals and demo tapes. The original bootleg CDs or LPs change hands for large amounts of money, but they can be downloaded in MP3 format free of charge. Of course, you cannot legally download any of these files. Nobody is likely to get into trouble for downloading them, but that doesn't make it any more legal. You should always ensure that you're entitled to own any files that you want to download.

Finding MP3s

Before you go looking for MP3 files, be sure that you understand the implications. Do not download any files unless you are entitled to do so.

MP3 Search

http://mp3.lycos.com

Famous ISP Lycos has teamed up with Fast (who also run the Lycos FTP search at http://ftpsearch.lycos.com) to produce this search engine. Most of the songs on it's database appear to be commercial ones, which raises major legal implications, but there is copyright free material too.

AudioGalaxy

http://www.audiogalaxy.com

This great site contains loads of information about the latest legal MP3 releases, which is a bit of a rarity. It also has the best search engine for any other files you might want.

MP3.com

http://www.mp3.com

MP3.com always stays abreast of the latest news and developments, and also contains lots of information about the latest legal MP3 releases. Also available are all of the

latest MP3 players and encoders. A really great site.

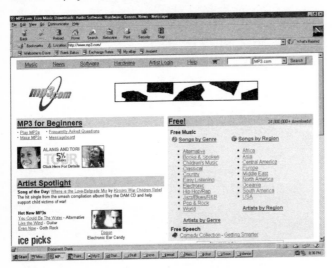

Making MP3s

Of course, you don't have to download MP3s - it's better in many cases to make your own instead. Encoding MP3s is a very processor-intensive activity, and you almost certainly won't be able to do much else with your computer whilst it's encoding. However, unless you have a very powerful ISDN connection it is unlikely to be quicker downloading the songs than creating them yourself!

One of the best encoders available is the XingMpeg Encoder. It encodes at a lightning rate, and is available from http://www.xing.com - as long as you're willing to pay for it. If you'd prefer one of the (usually slower) shareware encoders, then go to http://www.mp3.com, where all available encoders, (also called rippers), both shareware or commercial, are listed and rated.

WinAmp Extensions

There are many, many different independently made add-ons for WinAmp. The most popular are Skins. These are used to change the appearance of the program. You can make the WinAmp player look like anything from a Nokia mobile phone to a jukebox. The skins are all free, and you can find them on http://www.mp3.com.

		Rating
	Jesse's MP3.com Skin	★★★★★
	The best MP3.com-logo skin -- simple, smooth and not gaudy like some others. We doubt we'll see a better MP3.com skin anytime soon.	Size 75k
		Author Jesse Mellon & Sander van Zoest
	NokiAmp 1.0	Rating ★★★★★
	Has the same look and feel as Nokia products, such as their cell phones.	Size 33k
		Author ADN
	SketchAmp 1.1	Rating ★★★★★
	Only black and white and reminds of a kid's drawing... Certainly stands out from the rest.	Size 57k
		Author Sakamoto
	WITAMP jukebox 2.0	Rating ★★★★★
	Looks like a jukebox down to every detail. Colorful and cool.	Size 260k
		Author Michael Sos
	woodamp 1.0a	Rating ★★★★
	Had enough of high tech looking interfaces? Woodamp brings back the wood. Matching speakers plug-in is included.	Size 202k
		Author M. Bengtsson
	SpyAmp for winamp 2.x	Rating ★★★★
	This skin screams danger. Going for the slick thriller appeal.	Size 74k
		Author Unknown

Plugins are something else entirely. They usually add flash visual effects to the player. For example, some show elaborate 3D graphic equalisers, and some can be programmed to display the lyrics for a song (karaoke style). There is a huge range available, although you'll probably find that they become a bit annoying in a very short space of time, and you'll just turn them off.

Listening over the Internet

It is possible to stream MP3s over the Internet, as new site MY MP3 (http://my.mp3.com) shows. Using this site, it's possible to play your CD collection over the Internet, from any PC with Internet access. The trick is, you must 'Beam In' each of your CDs. Basically, their software examines your CD, and sends key information to MP3.com. This acts as proof that you actually own the CD. Then you can stream the tracks over the Internet and listen to them wherever you like. If you don't own the CDs, then you can order it from one of the online stores mentioned, and you will instantly be able to listen online. It's currently a free service, but that hasn't stopped the RIAA member companies from suing MP3.com for copyright violations. They say that encoding 40,000 CDs and putting them online for use in this fashion is an infringement on copyright. We don't know how the case will pan out, but it doesn't look too good for MP3.com at the moment. Still, it's a useful service and may pave the way for other licensed sites running along similar lines.

10 - Movies on your PC

The recent American cable-access boom has really shown us what the Internet is capable of. With 200k per second downloading gigantic video files is now easily possible, and as a result, you'll find more movies online than ever before.

Most of these movies are stored in MPEG format. This means that they're compressed - but not necessarily small. A decent quality movie lasting for ten seconds, with sound, can take up several megabytes of disk space. With this in mind, several companies have developed special formats to help keep size down.

Playing movies on your PC

The first PC video format was RealVideo (http://www.real.com). Using the Realplayer, you can view very highly compressed RealVideo files, but quality does suffer quite a bit. Images are usually slightly blocky, and motion is not captured extremely well in the higher compression ranges. It's fine for many uses, and is very popular, but it's quickly being overtaken by ASF. Real.com contains a large quantity of links containing RealAudio or Realvideo, in the form of an online directory.

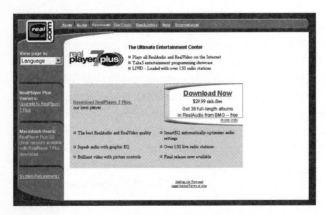

ASF is the new video format which is taking the online world by storm. It too is capable of tremendous compression, but the quality is much nicer. Using ASF, 140 minutes of video and sound can be compressed to a watchable level whilst taking up just 100

megabytes of disk-space. That's less than a meg a minute! Using ASF, you could fit fifteen hours of video onto a single CD!

Unfortunately, these new formats have bought with them a new wave of piracy, with thousands of people downloading the latest films often before they're released in this country.

Still, it's not all illegal - there's plenty of video out there for download. Check out such Newsgroups such as alt.binaries.multimedia for example.

One of the most frequently used video streaming sites is the news channel CNN (http://www.cnn.com/videoselect/) which offers videos of the latest stories for you to watch. You can view them in ASF, RealVideo or Quicktime, and at two different quality rates - one for 56k modems or less, and one for ISDN or above. Although much of the news is US-based, there's plenty of international stories to get your teeth into.

Virtue TV is another site which uses RealVideo, at http://www.virtuetv.com/. They offer plenty of footage on loads of different subjects - from news reports to full concerts. They also provide a radio station which plays hits from the Eighties. One to avoid there, then. The video is very good however, and contains much in the way of exclusive content - for example, at the time of writing there's an exclusive interview with Mel C. Better still, the concerts they provide are of excellent quality, and include class acts like Fatboy Slim and Travis. They're full concerts too, available free and on demand. All in all, it's brilliant - but a shame they only go up to 56k speeds, and there's no specific support for ISDN or faster connections. Everyone is limited to the same quality, which is dissapointing.

Obviously it's not at the peak of it's potential yet, but RealVideo and the other online formats do provide an interesting glimpse of the Internet as it will be in two years from now. When everybody has the ultra-fast ADSL or cable Internet connections, streaming incredibly high movies will be a part of every day Internet use for many people. Proper recorded Webcam footage may replace conventional text-based emails some day. For the time being, we're stuck with jerky, low-grade video, but that's set to change very soon.

11-Game Emulators

Have you ever wished that you could play your favourite console games on your PC? Ever wished you could play that old arcade game again that swallowed so many of your 10p coins in the early 80s? Well, the good news is that you probably can.

Emulation allows you to run software on your computer that was originally created for another. An emulator fools the software into thinking it's running on the system it was intended for by translating all of the instructions given into instructions that your PC can understand. Of course, it's quite a complicated procedure, and if you don't understand it, don't worry. Thankfully, using an emulator is a very, very simple task.

The early emulators existed only for Amigas, Atari STs and high-powered PCs - and they only allowed you to emulate the ancient Spectrum and C64 systems! These days, things have progressed a little. You can now play N64 or PlayStation games on your PC - and you don't even need any extra hardware!

Emulators are almost always freeware - you don't have to pay a penny. There are a few exceptions to this rule, but most of the best emulators are free. The software for emulated systems can also be downloaded online, but this isn't usually legal.

The reason we are covering emulation in an Internet book is that emulation is almost exclusively Internet based. It's a bit of a grey area as far as the law is concerned, so you hardly ever hear about emulators outside of the online world.

What you need
It depends. If you just want to run seventies and eighties arcade games, you can do so on a P90. But you'll need a slightly more powerful computer to emulate machines such

as the PlayStation. Emulation is a very processor-intensive activity, and you'll really need a P166 to run most decent emulators at full speed. Some emulators also require lots of RAM, though 32 Megabytes is usually sufficient.

Once you've got your emulator, you'll need some ROMs (or software) to run on it. Games are called ROMs because console or arcade games are always stored on little chips inside the machine or cart. These have to be downloaded from the Internet, unless you have a special piece of hardware that can read the carts or arcade boards into a computer. Note that downloading games is generally illegal, unless they are freely distributable.

Machines that can be emulated

This is a list of the main systems that can be emulated on the PC, and the software needed to emulate them. If you want to know about emulation on the Mac system, go to http://www.emulation.net. Note, those included here are only a few of the emulators available for each system. Most have many more available for them. The ones included in this list are usually (but not always) the best ones. If you want to download any of these emulators, simply go to http://www.vintagegaming.com (the world's best PC-based emulation site) and seek it out.

GameBoy	-	No$GB
Nintendo	-	Nesticle
SNES	-	ZSnes, Snes9X
N64	-	UltraHLE
PlayStation	-	Bleem!
Commodore 64	-	Frodo, Win64, C64s
Spectrum	-	Z80
Amiga (up to A500+)	-	UAE
Arcade games	-	MAME, Callus, Raine
Macintosh	-	Fusion
NeoGeo	-	NeoRage
MegaDrive	-	Genecyst
Master System	-	Massage
Atari Lynx	-	Handy
GameGear	-	Massage
Atari ST	-	PaCifiST

Arcade Games

Before moving onto the specifics of playing modern console games on your PC, we should look at the emulation of older games - or more specifically arcade games. In order to get games from arcade machines onto a computer, special hardware is needed. It reads the information from the ROM, and transfers it onto a computer.

The best emulator for arcade games has got to be MAME. It stands for Multiple Arcade Machine Emulator, and when it started it could only run a few games - Pacman being one of them. In the past few years however, it's grown and grown. It can now run around two thousand games including such classics as Golden Axe, Space Invaders, Moonwalker, Asteroids, Toobin', Mario Bros, Shadow Dancer, Outrun, Bomb Jack, The Simpsons, Teenage Mutant Ninja Turtles, Kick Off and Hang-On!

It's not just early eighties games either. Now it can run games as recent as StreetFighter II and beyond! MAME is written just written by one person. A number of people write emulation modules for individual arcade games, which are then compiled into one big program. This is how MAME has grown from a program that could emulate a tiny handful of ancient arcade games into the largest emulation project in the world, in the space of just a few years. If you remember an arcade game from the Eighties, it's probably going to be available in this emulator. It's fantastic.

The Win95 version of MAME is available from http://www.geocities.com/TimesSquare /Lair/8706/mame32.html. There are also versions available for Macs, Amigas, and most other operating systems. The games are available from various sites, but are still copyrighted, so they cannot legally be distributed. There are plenty of other arcade emulators out there, too, including Callus and the very capable Raine.

Computers

Most people in their twenties have memories of the ZX Spectrum and the C64. Many will have spent hours typing in huge program listings from magazines (which never worked). Well, now you can relive those early days of computing. Emulators for the C64 and Spectrum are plentiful, and they've had a long time to develop - they were amongst the first emulators to be made available. They're still not perfect, but they get better all the time.

One advantage of using these emulators is that the games are easily available. Strictly speaking, distribution of them is still illegal, but the companies who own the copyrights stopped catering for these systems years ago. Another advantage is that games for these systems are very small. They each download in just a few minutes - or often just a few seconds.

So why not give it a go? In a few minutes, you could be playing Jet Set Willy on your PC. Be warned though, playing old games is not as fun for as you remember - you'll probably begin to wonder why you ever wasted your time on such primitive entertainment.

Macintosh emulation is another matter entirely. Thanks to a program called Fusion, you can now emulate a Mac running OS 8! The Mac is the industry standard for design work, and buying Fusion can save you a lot of money over the cost of a real Mac. Unfortunately, Fusion only emulates the 680x0 range of processors (all modern Macs use Power PC processors), so a lot of modern software that needs the PPC processor won't work. It is said however that the programmers of Fusion are now working on PPC emulation - though they've been saying that for ages. Fusion is available for Mac and Amiga computers, and you can find its Web site at http://www.microcode-solutions.com/.

The Amiga was, and some might say still is, a very popular computer. They're still working on making entirely new Amigas at http://www.amiga.de, but if you just want to relive the nostalgia, then you can get hold of Amiga Forever. This is an entirely legal CD which contains the world's best Amiga emulator, UAE, and all of the required ROM files, along with some licenced commercial games and utilities! You can get the official CD from http://www.cloanto.com/amiga/forever/online.html. UAE itself however is free, and you can get it from http://www.codepoet.com/UAE/ or http://www.freiburg.linux.de/~uae/.

Early Consoles

It wasn't so long ago that everyone spent ages on the SNES and Megadrive consoles. Emulation has moved on a bit from SNES and Megadrive systems since they became more or less perfectly emulated. Most games can now be run on emulators such as GeneCyst and ZSnes, and the ROMs are reasonably plentiful on the Net. However, SNES emulation was the revolution that got Nintendo interested in emulation, or to be precise, interested in ending emulation. Nintendo have claimed that emulators are illegal, and they have been known to threaten legal action.

Modern Systems

The emulation of these systems has taken everyone by surprise. Both releases were at a time when nobody expected to be able to emulate these systems properly for at least a year - maybe two. They have certainly caused controversy, with the hardware manufacturers all throwing around threats of legal action.

N64/UltraHLE

http://www.ultrahle.com

This is the N64 emulator that took the world by storm. Days after its release, it was withdrawn because Nintendo didn't like it, and they promised legal action against the UltraHLE developers (which has yet to materialise). Nobody had expected to see any working Nintendo 64 emulators for at least a year, but UltraHLE really shook up the emulation community.

Unfortunately, N64 emulation is almost unavoidably illegal. This is because to emulate an N64, you have to own a copy of the game on your computer, which usually means that you will need to download the games from the Internet.

UltraHLE can run around 40 N64 games, with varying degrees of success. It was written primarily to run Goldeneye, Mario64, and Zelda. The fact that it can run other games is more or less coincidence. UltraHLE requires a 3DFX card to run, and it also needs a pretty fast processor. Mario64 is playable on a PII 266 machine with 3DFX . UltraHLE, now available as freeware once again, can be obtained from the official site.

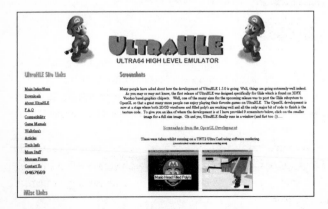

PSX/Bleem!

http://www.bleem.com

Bleem! was originally thought by many to be a hoax, but as it turns out, it's real. This was discovered after a beta (testing copy) of the program was leaked. Bleem! is now finished, and it can run most PlayStation games perfectly. It should run a lot of games well on only a P166, and on a PII 266 it can run games such as Resident Evil II at full speed. It plays movies and CD sound - and it doesn't need a 3D card. Of course, if you do have a 3D card, then you can certainly see the benefits. The jury is still out on whether Playstation emulation is legal, since you have to use original PlayStation software. You just stick the CD into the drive, and you're away.

A demo of Bleem! is available for PC users at http://www.bleem.com. Unfortunately, it's crippled - and the full version costs around $39 (about £25). Mac users can try Virtual Gamestation at http://www.virtualgamestation.com

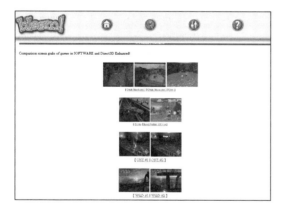

Resources

If you want to learn more about emulation, check out http://www.emux.com, or check out the newsgroups. One of the main emulation groups is comp.emulators.misc.

Search engines such as AltaVista (http://www.altavista.com) will prove very useful for anyone wanting to emulate systems of any sort. Use your common sense when searching, and you're bound to find what you want. Newsgroups also exist which carry emulators and the software to run on them.

12-Your Own Website

When you've been surfing for a while, you might decide that you'd like to add your own contribution to the World Wide Web. Thankfully, creating a Web site is very easy. You need to learn a bit of HTML (HyperText Markup Language), but apart from that it's a doddle. You can create a Web site about almost anything. It could be about your favourite band, your favourite author - or it could be more general. A site containing film or music reviews, for example - it's up to you.

Where to put it

Your ISP will probably have provided you with some space on their own server. For information on how to access it, you'll have to check your ISP's Website. However, it almost always involves FTP, so make sure you've read the chapter concerning FTP in this book.

If your ISP doesn't give you any (or enough) disk space, then there are plenty of places to get it online. You could always sign up with an ISP such as UKOnline, which provides unlimited diskspace, or check out one of the following free providers. Remember that free providers have to make money somehow - and often this can be by forcing you to include advertising on your Website.

Geocities

http://www.geocities.com

Geocities is the most famous Web provider in the world, with millions of satisfied users. Unfortunately it finances itself by using your Website as a showcase for it's advertisers. Still, you get 10 Megs, and a reliable service. All Web sites are put into categories and sub-categories, which means that your URL can be very long indeed. A free email account is also supplied.

Fortune City

http://www.fortunecity.com

Based in the UK, FortuneCity also offers you 10 Megs of space. The site, like Geocities, is very popular, and has an additional advantage of increased speed over Geocities. In many respects the choice comes down to whether you want to have a Geocities or Fortune City site.

Xoom

http://www.xoom.com

Xoom is a pretty bog standard provider. They offer unlimited disk space, but they are unusually picky about the content of the Web pages on their servers. MP3 files (even those that are legal) are banned from their servers.

All of the above providers require that you use FTP to access them properly. Still, many also contain site-building pages, which allow you to build a simple site without FTP. They contain detailed usage information on their Websites, so you really can't go wrong with them.

How to write it

This is the difficult part - learning HTML. This book couldn't possibly instruct you on the ins and outs of Web Site creation - but we can give you enough information to create a reasonably decent site.

You'll need the tools of the trade - firstly, a decent text editing program. Anything will do - even Wordpad (which is supplied with Windows) works well, and a graphics editing tool. After all, how many Web sites do you know of that don't have any pictures? If you're rich, you could use the brilliant Photoshop (http://www.adobe.com)- easily the best choice - but if you're on a budget you could use a program such as Paint Shop Pro. PSP, available from http://www.psp.com, is one of the most popular shareware programs of all time. It offers many of the same features as Photoshop. The results are rarely as impressive, but it's a good budget option.

These are the main elements that you'll need. But the difficult part is yet to come -

learning HTML.

HTML

HTML isn't a programming language - it's just a way of formatting text. An HTML document is nothing more than a plain text file. You can view an HTML file in Notepad or Wordpad, but it'll look a bit confusing at first.

An HTML document contains the text that you want on your page, interspersed with lots of control codes. The Web browser will be looking for these control codes when it displays a page - otherwise it'll be shown as a simple page full of text. These control codes have to do everything - from making links to starting a new paragraph.

Control codes (from now on known as 'tags') are always contained within angle brackets (these <> things). These tags are inserted in and around the text, and if you look at the source code behind a page (go to the 'View' menu and select 'Page Source'), you'll see what we mean - and it can be quite confusing. It isn't that bad however, and once you understand what each tag does, it'll become crystal clear.

Tags are usually used in pairs. For example:

<b> this text would be bold </b>

The <b> tells the browser that all following text is to be displayed in bold. The </b> tells the browser that the bold text ends at that point.

That much is easy to grasp. Here are some other simple tags that work along very similar lines:

Start Tag	Action	End Tag
<i>	Present all following text in italics.	</i>
<u>	Underline all following text.	</u>
<p>	Start a paragraph	</p>
<h1>	Header text - different numbers make different sizes.	</h1>
<html>	Put at the start (and at the end) of each HTML document.	</html>
<center>	Puts all text in the centre of the window.	</center>

So you can see how tags work at their most basic. Perhaps the best way to illustrate how the other tags would be to do so in the context of examining a simple piece of HTML, which we'll do now.

Before we start, however, you should know that HTML documents don't have to be formatted well - for example:

This is a line of text.

...would work in exactly the same way as this:

this is a line of text.

The extra line in the first example would be ignored. You could do your entire page as one big block of text if you wanted to, the results would still be the same. Most people like to space things out a bit to make the pages easier to edit, and we've done this to an extent below.

The following is a simple example. You can look upon it as a worse-case scenario. Your attempt could not possibly be worse than Harry's one. The finished page is on the right - to help see what it is we're working towards. You can also see it online in its full glory if you point your browser towards http://www.fkbonline.co.uk/harry/.

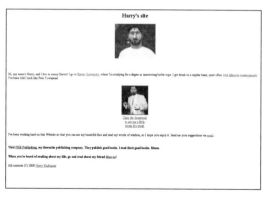

OK, now let's see how that site was put together.

— html begins—
<html>

<title>My Page</title>

<body bgcolor="#FFFFFF"> **[sets the background colour to white]**

<center>

<h1>Harry's site</h1> **[designates that this text is a heading]**

<img SRC="portrait2.JPG"> **[inserts an image]**

</center>

<p>

<font face="Verdana"><font size=-1>Hi, my name's Harry, and I live in
sunny Exeter! I go to <a href="http://www.exeter.ac.uk">Exeter University</a> **[These
tags make the words 'Exeter University' a link to the Exeter University Website]**,
where I'm studying for a degree in unscrewing bottle tops. I get drunk on a regular
basis, quite often <a href="http://www.altavista.com/cgi-
bin/query?pg=q&sc=on&hl=on&q=%22with+hilarious+consequences">with
hilarious consequences</a> **['with hilarious consequences' is made into a link]**. I've
been told I look like Pete Townsend.

</font></font>**[Turn off those font changes we made]**

<center>
<p>
<a href="beermonster.JPG"><img SRC="beermonster_thumb.JPG" height=106
width=100></a> **[This is, as you can see, similar to a normal link – except the link
isn't text, it's an image. We simply shrunk the image in a paint program and used
it as a thumbnail. The visitor then clicks the smaller image to view the full sized
one]**

118

<font face="Verdana"><font size=-2><a href="beermonster.JPG">Click the
thumbnail to see me a little worse for wear!</a></font></font></center>

<p><font face="Verdana"><font size=-1>I've been working hard on this Website
so that you can see my beautiful face and read my words of wisdom, so I
hope you enjoy it. Send me your suggestions via <a
href="mailto:osiris@eidosnet.co.uk">email</a> **[As you can see, this is a normal
text link, but the 'mailto' part replacing 'http://' designates the link as an email
address – when you click it, your email program will open up a blank,
preaddressed email so that you can email Harry!]**.

</font></font>

<p>

<b><font face="Verdana"><font size=-1>Visit <a
href="http://www.fkbonline.co.uk">FKB
Publishing</a>, my favourite publishing company. They publish good books.
I read their good books. Mmm.</font></font></b>

<p>

<b><font face="Verdana"><font size=-1>When you're bored of reading about
my life, go and read about my friend <a
href="http://books.mirror.org/gb.aurelius.html">Marcus</a>!</font></font></b>

<p><font face="Verdana"><font size=-2>All contents (C) 2000 <a
href="mailto:osiris@eidosnet.co.uk">Harry
Hadrianus</a></font></font>

<font face="Verdana"><font size=-2></font></font>

</body>
</html>
—ends—

Now, that Web site would win no design awards, and it certainly wouldn't win any awards for the quality of the HTML programming! Any HTML expert would probably be able to find a dozen or more faults with that HTML - but the point is, as long as it works, that's all that matters. Most Web sites are amateur efforts, and hardly anybody knows HTML well enough to do a perfect site. There are all manner of rules that you should follow when writing HTML, but at the end of the day, they're rather unimportant.

Of course, we didn't cover things such as frames, tables or Javascript - those are things you'd have to find out about yourself!

The Easy Way

If you can't be bothered with all of that HTML rubbish, then you could always get one of the wealth of WYSIWYG (What You See Is What You Get) editors. Unfortunately, most of these editors also require at least a little knowledge of HTML. Many HTML purists don't like these programs, and they are quite often expensive for what they provide.

Netscape Communicator

http://www.netscape.com

Communicator comes complete with Composer, a cheap and cheerful program for the creation of Websites. It's an effective piece of work, and can make life much easier for you. As free WYSIWYG editors go, it's probably the best.

HotDog Pro

http://www.sausage.com.au

HotDog has been around for years, and it's developed into a very capable piece of software. It's quite expensive, but it's worth the money if you do decide that you need some authoring software. A shareware version of HotDog is available, if you'd like to try it out first.

FrontPage

http:///www.microsoft.com

FrontPage is a typical Microsoft program in that it's mind-bogglingly easy to use. Anyone can get started with FrontPage, and it's probably one of the best programs for the amateur or semi-professional Web site designer.

HoTMetaLPRO

http://www.softquad.com/i

HotMetal offers many professional features, and, like HotDog, it's been around for a while. There is an evaluation version available for download.

Dreamweaver
http://www.dreamweaver.com
Immensely powerful and remarkably easy to use, Dreamweaver is a Webmaster's dream. Unfortunately, most of us can only dream of being able to afford it.

Design tips
* It's no good learning HTML if you're going to produce the sort of page that nobody will want to read. The design of a Web site is often directly related to it's success or failure. Follow these handy tips if you want to get ahead in the Web design stakes.

* Be sensible with the colours that you use. Don't go mad with reds and yellows!

* Don't be tempted to fill the page with huge images - nobody likes a site that takes ages to load.

* Never, ever include MIDI files on your Website - too many people do it already! We're basically talking about a Web page that starts playing an awful plinky-plonky little tune through your soundcard. If you do this, you probably need a hearing aid.

* Use frames wisely. Many people use too many frames, and it gets confusing.

* When linking to an external site within a frame, make sure that the link opens a new browser window for the link - don't let the external site load into one of your frames - that's very annoying.

* Use smallish text. A page full of huge text is very hard on the eyes! If you use a background image, try to find or create one that's in greyscale, and make sure the brightness of the image is turned up, and the contrast is turned down. That way it can still be seen, but it is never darker than the text, and exhibits a very nice 'watermark' effect - rather than making your eyes hurt.

* Transparent gifs are often used to good effect. They are like normal pictures, but one of the colours (usually the background colour) is transparent. This means that you could

have a photo of an object, but the space around the picture shows the background image instead of white.

* Don't go overboard on the amount of fonts you use when creating images for your site. Two different fonts are usually more than enough, and make sure you only use standard ones. Otherwise, the chances are that your readers won't have the same ones as you do!

General tips

* If you think your site is worth it, then submit it to as many search engines as you can. Go to the homepage of each search engine and try to find out how to add your site to it. Particularly important is to add your site to Yahoo (http://www.yahoo.com).

* Make sure your site is going to interest people. Too many people put up a dull site that lists their friends, hobbies and their pet's names. Nobody will want to read that stuff, unless they're stalking you.

* Be careful about breaking copyright laws. Several companies, including Sony and 20th Century Fox have proven their ability to bully Web site owners into removing things such as song lyrics and pictures from their Web sites - or else. This may not be commendable behaviour on the part of the companies involved, but unfortunately if it came to a court case, they'd probably be able to afford solicitors that could convince the court that black was white. You wouldn't stand much of a chance, basically.

* Don't link to anything that contains something illegal. It's been proven in court that linking to an illegal Web site can be considered to be the same as 'publishing' the material! This may be outrageous, but that's the way it goes.

* Don't fall into the trap of including endless amounts of gimmicky Java. It can really slow down a Web site.

* Including a Guestbook can be useful. People can leave feedback, be it either encouragement or constructive criticism. You can get a free Guestbook from http://www.alxbook.com/. In a similar vein, try and encourage people to email you with their comments.

* Starting a small mailing list can help to keep your visitors updated on the latest news. Go to http://www.listbot.com/ for a free solution.

13 - Promoting business online

Almost all businesses could benefit from a bit of online promotion, but you must always ensure that you take the right approach. If you act irresponsibly, you'll suffer the consequences, since Internet marketing is a touchy subject amongst Internet users.

Walking the tightrope

Of course, nobody will worry if you set up a Web site to advertise your business. Indeed, that's going to be welcomed by all. However, it's when email and Newsgroups start to become involved in the process of marketing that problems tend to occur. The Internet is becoming more commercial every day, but you must take care not to invade the public sectors, which will earn you hatred and scorn rather than increased custom.

Setting up

Once you're online, it can be a bit bewildering, and you may find it difficult to know where to start. The best thing to do would be to work out your budget. If you're serious about setting up online, you'll probably need around £150 to begin with. You'll need to purchase a domain name (companyname.co.uk, probably) which will set you back around £25 (possibly less) and the Web space. You could probably get that for around £15 per month, with most of the trimmings you'll need.

You can get a good domain-hosting service provided free by the free-ISP Freeola, http://www.freeola.com, as part of their service. It's very nifty, doesn't cost a penny, and there are no advertising banners either. You could certainly do a lot worse. Be warned, however, Freeola have had some technical difficulties in the past, which has left customers stranded for days at a time without access to their email or websites, with little or no explanation or warning. Technical support is also charged at premium rate prices.

123

Anyway, for the prices outlined you get a Website hosted with the address http://www.whateveryouwant.co.uk. That doesn't include Web design, which is best done yourself, unless you either have a heck of a lot of money to spend or if you don't mind it being completely useless. Do not get cheap and cheerful designers to work on a site, they're almost always completely useless, and often rather lacking in the brains department. Doing it yourself is a good option, as long as you have at least some sense of style. If you want to use a load of Microsoft clip-art then that's a good indication that you probably shouldn't bother.

Obviously, you probably won't have the resources of the big-boys, and you don't want your small home business to be turned into the next Amazon.com - that would probably mean more work than you're accustomed to. However, you can certainly make a simple site look clear and presentable.

Designing a site

We've prepared two example Websites, which show the wrong way and the right way to go about putting a small business online. One shows all of the worst elements of homespun Webpages, whilst the other - still very far from being perfect - at least shows a degree of restraint and a desire for the site to be easy to navigate. In each case, only the homepage (index.html) has been created.

Firstly, let's take a look at the ugly site, which can be found online at http://www.fkbonline.co.uk/hell/. It's advertising Ovid's Office Supplies LTD, and as you'll see, poor Ovid has proven himself a worthy candidate for a good whipping. Here are just some of the problems with his page:

* Flashing text.
* Red text on a black background
* Spurious use of clip-art
* Awful grammar
* Use of the > character as an indentation, instead of bullet points.

You'll probably be able to find more problems yourself. It's a dreadful page, but not unrealistic. There are many pages online which are just as bad, or even worse! You're bound to come across some on your travels.

However, if you want to see an example of a far more reasonable page, created with the same limited resources and the same software, then point your browser at http://www.fkbonline.co.uk/heaven/.

This site is far from becoming the next Amazon.com, but it has been executed with a small amount of restraint and dignity. It's obviously a much nicer site, and didn't take that much longer to achieve either. Here are some of the advantages to Fred's approach:

* Nicer, softer colours, making text easy to read.
* Good grammar and spelling.
* Nice, clean images.

* Contact details clearly visible.
* Photo of dealer included - customers like to know whom they're dealing with, though this is down to personal preference.
* Payment methods clearly stated.

It's obviously a great improvement, and it's a standard easily obtainable by anybody with a copy of Netscape Communicator and a simple graphics program. If you want to see how it was done, feel free to view the HTML source and rip it off, though you could do something a lot better yourself. That site simply illustrates what can be achieved in 30 mins with copies of Paintshop Pro & Netscape Communicator.

Promoting your site

Once you've got your Webpage up and running, there are other things you'll need to do. Firstly, you might want to put your Web and email address on your business card. This is very important, and you mustn't underestimate the importance of doing it. Secondly, you'll want to add the site to Yahoo. Instructions for doing so can be found on the Yahoo homepage (http://www.yahoo.co.uk). Make sure you put it in an appropriate category, and provide a good, catchy description for the site. Yahoo can pull in thousands of hits, and should not be overlooked.

Then, contact Webmasters of appropriate sites and see if they'll accept reciprocal links. Many will gladly link to your page if you link to them in return. Email appropriate news-based sites and hopefully they'll cover your launch (though don't expect CNN to be interested in your online paperclip emporium). All of these things help to get your site exposure, which is what it all comes down to at the end of the day.

There are two things you must never, ever do. Firstly, don't ever send out unsolicited emails advertising your site. It does not matter who tells you it's okay, it does not matter how many people could benefit from your site - if you send spam out to people, you'll deserve everything you get! Junk mail may be grudgingly accepted in real life, but people are certainly not so forgiving online. If you send unsolicited email, you will be tracked down, and your ISP will immediately ban you from using their services. Spammers, when tracked down, routinely receive death threats and have their companies ruined, so it's probably not the wisest choice. Obviously, the same applies to Newsgroup posts.

Newsgroups can be very helpful to business, but you have to do it carefully. Try putting the URL of your business into your signature (see email chapter on page XX), and then making helpful posts into appropriate groups. Answer people's questions and make yourself known. If you appear knowledgeable and friendly, people will probably visit your site of their own accord. Don't, however, answer someone's question and then say '... by the way, visit my Website! Lots of bargains and 25% off everything!'. That's bad, and people will soon realise that you're only posting for your own benefit. A signature such as this will do the job a thousand times better:

Paul Bartlett
Teaboy in chief, FKB Publishing, Publishers of fine Internet books.
http://www.fkbonline.co.uk

That's easily adaptable for other uses, and does the job admirably. Much better than blatant advertising ever would.

Still, you should try and get into the spirit of the group, don't just post for your own reasons. Naturally, don't participate in arguments (and if they affect you, back out immediately) to avoid giving your business a bad name. Newsgroups can be brilliant ways to make new contacts in whatever industry you belong.

Web Site Guide

The size and ever changing nature of the World Wide Web makes it an impossible task to compile the perfect directory of sites. However the following section presents a broad range of the best sites. Most of them will also contain links to many other sites with related subject matter making them a good starting point.

In order to bring a sense of structure the sites have been categorised into sections. With sites that cover many possible areas within the headings listed, you may have to hunt about sometimes to track down what you are looking for.

To open any of the sites just type their address (in lower case), into the address window at the top of your browser. With some more up to date browsers you may be able to get away without typing the http:// part as they will assume this is part of the address. If you like the site once it is open then you can make it a bookmark or favourite. You will then be able to jump to the site without having to type it out again next time.

All the sites in this guide have been researched and checked. The nature of the web is such that you will almost certainly find some of them no longer exist or have moved elsewhere. Unfortunately that's the way it is with fast moving technol   ogy. You can however use a Search Engine for lost sites and often find them in different locations.

Art	130	Magazines	184
Astronomy	130	Music	186
Auctions	132	Nature and pets	189
Beer	133	News	191
Betting	134	Online Gaming	192
Books	135	Parenting	195
Business and Finance	136	Pop Culture	195
Camping and Caravanning	140	Property	198
Comedy	141	Psychic	199
Comics	143	Reference	200
Computing	144	Religion	203
Dating	146	Science	204
Dictionaries	147	Science Fiction	206
Downloading	148	Search Engines	207
Ecology	149	Shopping	208
Employment	152	Sport	215
Extreme Sports	153	Strange	218
Fashion	155	Technology	220
Films	157	Television and Radio	222
Food and Drink	160	Theatre and Performing Arts	226
Football	163	Transport	228
Games	165	Travel	229
Government	166	Weather	235
Health and Fitness	168	Web Broadcasting	236
History	174	Web Cameras	238
Hobbies and pastimes	175	Web Design	240
Kids	177	Weekends and Days Out	241
Language	183		

Art

Collage
http://collage.nhil.com/
Browse through with the opportunity of buying over 20,000 works from the Guildhall Library and Art Gallery in London.

The Creative Nude and Photographic Network
http://www.ethoseros.com/cnpn.html
If arty black and white photography of the erotic nature is up your street check out this site. Far from being an excuse for showing lots of female flesh, it is actually very well done and very tasteful.

Glasgow School of Art
http://www.gsa.ac.uk
A beautifully made site with loads of Charles Rennie Mackintosh. Work from recent students is also interesting.

The National Gallery
http://www.nationalgallery.org.uk
Highlights of new and recent exhibitions rather than the full 2000 plus paintings. Also information about the museum all in a clear simple site.

Louvre Museum
http://mistral.culture.fr/louvre/louvrea.htm
Stunning to look at, this site more than lives up to its appearance. Photographs of some fantastic exhibits, a journey around the museum, current and upcoming special exhibitions and opening hours.

Tate Gallery
http://www.tate.org.uk
Very well made and detailed site featuring the General Collection, the Oppe Collection and New Acquisitions, all online at various resolutions.

The Teletubbies Gallery of Fine Arts *
http://www.slacker.clara.net/teletubbies
View peoples lame efforts at drawing Teletubbies. Quite bizzare.

Astronomy

Astro Info
http://www.astroinfo.ch
"Astronomical information in Cyberspace". Daily updates site with

many links to publications. Contains a gallery of pictures of various astronomical bodies/events catalogued by time and location.

The Best of Hubble
http://www.seds.org/hst/
The Hubble had a troubled start to life, but once everything was corrected the results gleaned from it were truly amazing. Check out some of them here.

Galaxies *
http://zebu.uoregon.edu/galaxy.html
This archive site offers good quality photographs and images of galaxies, along with links and educational resources.

IAU
http://www.iau.org
The International Astronomical Union. Includes news, events, research, member details and other information.

Mars Polar Explorer *
http://mars.pgd.hawaii.edu/default1.html
Stunning pictures of the martian landscape are viewable from this site. Along with the Explorers holiday snaps there is also some intelligent discussion of the images portrayed.

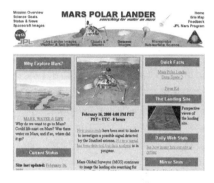

NASA Office of Space Science
http://spacescience.nasa.gov/
Check this site out for some stunning photos of the earth as taken by various probes. Information on the technology used to create such images is provided.

NASA
http://www.nasa.gov
The NASA homepage. Includes a huge amount of links to research centres, space flight, galactic anomalies, teaching, technology and astronomy.

The Planetary Society
http://www.planetary.org/
Far from being another paranoid UFO site, this offers intelligent discussion and

informative text about the ongoing quest to find life outside of the Earth.

The Sky at Night

http://www.bbc.co.uk/skyatnight
Very slick site featuring the indomitable Patrick Moore. With news, history, events, glossaries and quiz pages. A must see.

SOHO

http://sohowww.nascom.nasa.gov
Both NASA and the ESA are responsible for this project which seeks to find out more information about our nearest star, the Sun. Some interesting text and images provide a truly fascinating site.

Welcome to the Planets

http://pds.jpl.nasa.gov/planets
This site centres on our local solar system. With pictures of all of the planets and figures on them to compare and contrast, this is a great place to go planet hopping.

Auctions

Blue Cycle

http://www.bluecycle.com
Blue Cycle, set up by CGU, auctions all manner of goods - much of it recovered stolen property. If you want a pair of dirty old shovels or a tatty old Barry Manilow cassette, you know where to go.

eBay *

http://www.ebay.com
What can be said about the best public auction site in the world? Based in the US, but with a real worldwide community spirit. Buy anything from beanie bears to books, clothes, music, computers and the fingers of ancient Egyptian mummies. It's all on eBay.

eHay

http://www.hecklers.com/ehay/index.html
An amusing redneck version of famous auction site eBay. Git on there an' sell more thangs!

QXL

http://www.qxl.co.uk
QXL offer a huge range of UK-based auctions, some of which are run by QXL themselves, some of which are run by companies and individuals. Often a bargain to be had!

Beer

Bemish

http://www.beamish.ie

Purveyors of genuine Irish stout for over 200 years, this site documents the company's history, including pictures to inspire.

BreWorld *

http://www.breworld.com

European centre for beer and brewing. Fascinating site for both the industry and home brewers alike. It offers information on events, news, organisations, and the perfect ingredients needed for that extra-special pint.

Welcome to breWorld
breWorld is Europe's largest Internet site dedicated to the brewing industry.
You will find breWorld an invaluable source of news, information and entertainment regarding the brewing industry. Subscribe to the breWorld news letter to keep on top of the drinks industry.

www.breworld.net - Free Internet Access.
An Internet first, free Internet access with no strings attached. No monthly fee, local rate phone calls, easy and quick installation. breWorld.NET will bring the world of beer and brewing to your home page. breWorld.NET offers their subscribers exclusive information, competitions and much more.

www.beersite.com
Fed up with using those large search engines ? Search a key word and get back 30,000 sites, 25,000 of which are totally unrelated ?
The search engine for the brewing industry has arrived. Consisting of

Budweiser

http://www.budweiser.com

Come to the home of the battling reptiles and see the ever popular American lager in all its glory. Find out about the company history, and even get I.D'ed on the way in!

CAMRA

http://www.camra.org.uk

The Campaign for Real Ale's homepage. Includes links to pubs, tourist information, associated lobby groups, news, and a good beer guide amongst other beer related topics.

Fosters

http://www.fostersbeer.com

Learn how to throw shrimps on barbies with this bonza Website's Australian lessons, then get to grips with the history of the amber nectar.

Fuller Smith and Turner

http://www.fullers.co.uk

Facts about Fullers real ales with information on where to drink them.

Guinness *

http://www.guinness.ie

This site features all the history of this famous beverage, as well as games, lifestyle tips, and humour. Not quick to load.... but worth waiting for.

The Good Pub Guide

http://www.goodguides.com/
pubs/search.asp

The online version of The Good Pub Guide detailing pubs in England, Wales and Scotland recommended for their food, drink or accommodation.

Portman Group

http://www.portman-group.org.uk

A site which tries to prevent misuse of alcohol and promote sensible drinking.

Young and Co's Brewery

http://www.youngs.co.uk

All the facts you need about Young's real ales. Also details of all the Young's pubs and hotels.

Betting

Blue Square

http://www.bluesq.com

Fancy a bit of online betting? A fancy site which is quick and easy to use - but don't go mad!

Champion Tips

http://www.championtips.com

Don't trust your own judgement? Then use Champion Tips to decide which bets to put on instead.

Ladbrokes

http://www.ladbrokes.co.uk

The Ladbrokes betting site has lots of football news, in addition to the ability to bet online. It doesn't look as nice as some of the other sites, but it's clean and functional.

Racing Post

http://www.racingpost.co.uk

One of the definitive magazines for gamblers everywhere, the Racing Post has a decent site with loads of news, updated daily.

Totalbet *

https://www.totalbet.com

Tote and the Sporting Life have this online betting offering, which, as usual, allows you to spend online with your credit card.

William Hill

http://www.williamhill.co.uk

Similar in many ways to Blue Square, William Hill allows you to squander your hard-earned cash online with your credit card. Loads of info, and always tax-free.

Books

•••••••••••••••••••••••••••••

Amazon *
http://www.amazon.co.uk
Amazon is touted as the worlds biggest bookshop and can offer you a huge range of titles to buy online. You can use the company's own well developed search-engine to find books and build your own online book store by becoming an Amazon associate.

Bookends
http://www.bookends.co.uk
Excellent online magazine with news, reviews, links to bookshops, events and authors. Also features guest columnists and storywriters.

The British Library
http://www.bl.uk
Information about the library's

collections and services, along with the document catalogue, current serial databases and connection to the Gabriel network of pan-European library databases.

Computer Books
http://www.compman.co.uk
If you want PC books then this is a great site that carries most titles in stock for immediate despatch. You can find all the FKB books here!

Discworld
http://www.us.lspace.org
A Terry Pratchett/ Discworld site, containing a wealth of information for fans of the Discworld novels.

Waterstones
http://www.waterstones.co.uk
Good site with news and information on topical events. You can search the database by a number of criteria for books that are currently in or out of print.

Business and Finance

Abbey National Direct
http://www.abbeynational.co.uk
Need to take some money out but don't know where the nearest machine is? This site will let you know. You can also get in touch with your bank via email.

Alliance and Leicester
http://www.alliance-leicester.com
From the comfort of your own PC this site allows you to apply for a savings account, credit cards and mortgages.

American Express
http://www.americanexpress.com
Whether you're a customer or not, this site could prove of interest. If you haven't got one you can apply for a card. If you have a card already you can contact customer services, get a statement, and check your account balance online.

Barclays Stockbrokers
http://www.barclays-stockbrokers.co.uk
An online stockbroking service from Barclays, providing helpful advice and a real time dealing service.

Bloomberg
http://www.bloomberg.co.uk
This news-oriented site carries all of the main currencies, "hot stocks", FTSE 100 share index information, and links to the other global Bloomberg sites.

Business Wire
http://www.businesswire.com
A convenient way to keep track of how your company is doing. View news as it happens by headlines or full stories, browse through industry specific stories and gather top stories by date or period.

Charles Schwab *
http://www.charlesschwab.com
Daunting to anyone who knows nothing about the subject. It is highly professional, and will really appeal to anyone with a real interest in finance and the money markets.

Calculator
http://www.financenter.com/calcs.html
Although a U.S based site, this invaluable resource offers over 10 categories to build a calculator to work out all of your financial sums and forecasts.

Citibank *

http://www.citibank.co.uk

Using one of the worlds best known banks you can view up to 90 days worth of transactions, view balances, transfer funds, pay and cancel bills and even set up and pay standing orders.

CyberSpace Law Centre

http://cyber.findlaw.com

Lots of things on the Internet are not covered by laws of censorship, copyright and so on, purely because the Web is still so young. This site has gathered what information there is, and presented it in an easy to understand manner.

The Deal

http://www.thedeal.net

A financial lifestyle magazine that doesn't bore the pants off you. Home improvement, mortgages, holidays and other content for everyone, rich or... er... rich.

Dow Jones

http://www.dowjones.com

A huge and complete financial news service the lets you tailor the news you receive to your own needs. Plus information on over 10 million companies.

Egg *

http://www.egg.co.uk

Providing internet friendly savings accounts, loans and credit cards. Plus the Egg-free zone, which provides independent financial advice and opinions.

Electronic Share Information

http://www.esi.co.uk/

If you fancy a bit of share dealing over the Internet, you now know where to come. Also find out how much certain shares are worth and get information on the companies you want to invest in.

Fidelity UK

http://www.fidelity.co.uk

This redesigned site provides a broad selection of information on investments.

Market information is included here as well as interactive tolls and product details.

FinanceWise *

http://www.financewise.com

Containing a bookshop for financial information in addition to comprehensive company data.

Financial Network

http://cnnfn.com

This CNN site enables you to trade 24 hours a day and gives you up to date worldwide financial information. A well respected site.

The Financial Mail on Sunday

http://www.financialmail.co.uk/

This offers more accessible reading of the current financial state of affairs. Easier to use than many others, it is a great site for those with little or no knowledge of the subject matter.

Financial Times

http://www.ft.com/

Although first time users must register to this site, its European news, online prices, articles and interviews are all very worthwhile. There is information on almost all the markets, as well as a "quick view" page, for anyone in a hurry!

Interactive Investor International

http://www.iii.co.uk

Financial news, tips and advice for investors. Includes special offers and personalised portfolios.

Loan Company

http://www.loancorp.co.uk/

If you require a rapid injection of cash, have a look at this site and see if there is anything they can offer you. That car and holiday can be yours!

London Stock Exchange *

http://www.londonstockexchange.com

Current figures on the stock exchange can be found here as well as some interesting biography. Learn about our historic financial figurehead and how you can use it. For the beginners there's a dictionary here too.

Lombard
http://www.lombard.com
Lombard offer a direct trading service for everything from stocks to mutual fund investments, subject to membership. This service is backed up by comprehensive online news and free unlimited use of their online quotation service.

Nasdaq *
http://www.nasdaq.com/
No round up of finance related sites would be complete without this site. Almost everything is offered here, all with sound impartial advice. It is an expansive site and includes investment tutorials and an online library. A must see.

Nationwide *
http://www.nationwide.co.uk
Not only do Nationwide allow you to look

after your finances with the click of a mouse. It also provides some excellent links in a very user friendly site.

Natwest
http://www.natwest.co.uk
As well as the standard customer services that are available through this site, there are services and advice sections for doctors, solicitors and more besides. A very user friendly site offering lots of information.

Screentrade
http://www.screentrade.co.uk/
This site claims to be all you need for getting a quote for all kinds of insurance, be it car, home or travel.

Red Herring
http://www.redherring.com/
Another site devoted to various financial happenings around the world. The usual figures, company reports and backgrounds are available, on a slightly more accessible site.

139

The Stock Club

http://www.stockclub.com

This uncomplicated site is an extremely useful discussion point for all aspects of stocks and investment. You can choose to enter discussions about your favourite topics and even be notified directly by email if any of your subjects are being discussed.

The Inland Revenue

http://www.inlandrevenue.gov.uk/home.htm

Oh well, it had to happen sooner or later, I knew I should have kept those receipts! On a more serious note, the infamous office are here to help with clear advice and postings on pertinent dates on the tax calendar, along with a tax office database. Don't panic!

Visa

http://www.visa.com

With the Internet now a truly pervasive technology, actual cash changing hands could well be on the slide. Visa wants to be there when it starts to happen. Check this site out for card holder services and promotions.

Wall Street City

http://www.wallstreetcity.com

This site leads you around the inevitable minefield that is investing on the Internet. It lets you know where the soundest deals are to be had, although

nothing of course is guaranteed.

The Wall Street Journal*

http://www.wsj.com/

A good, uncomplicated and extensive site which in addition to all the monetary information gives you advice on how to start up in business. Business travel guides are here too.

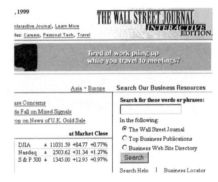

Camping and Caravaning

Best of British *

http://www.bob.org.uk/

The Best of British camping and caravan parks. This invaluable site links the UK's best campsites, with a commitment to quality and reliability of service for its patrons.

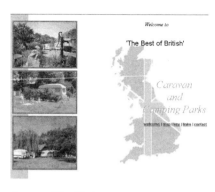

Welcome to
'The Best of British'

Caravan
and
Camping Parks

welcome | map | links | contact

Caravan Site finder

http://www.caravan-sitefinder.co.uk/
A well maintained directory site
containing lists of regional caravan sites
with information to help plan your
holiday.

The Caravan Club *

http://www.caravanclub.co.uk/
Official multilingual site available for
both members and non-members alike,
with comprehensive links and
information about the club and its
affiliated sites and organisations.

Comedy

. . . .

AAA Jokes Server

http://www.jokeserver.com
Thousands of jokes covering a wide range
of subjects. You can join a mailing list to
receive a joke a day, and email any that
you think are particularly funny to
friends. Beware if you are easily offended.

Bert Is Evil

http://www.fortunecity.com/bennyhills/
murphy/259/bert.htm/
Fantastic site dedicated to the truth
about sesame street's supposed do-
gooder. More controversial than
watergate, the megalomaniacal
dictatorship this once loveable character
is trying to create must be stopped at all
costs. Scandalous!

Comedy Channel

http://www.aentv.com/home/
chcomedy.htm/
This site offers both recorded and live
stand up routines from some excellent
comedians, from slapstick to alternative.

Daniel Flower Joke Site

http://homepages.ihug.co.nz/~drflower/
jokes/
A selection of the most awful and
appalling jokes possible. The site splits
into general, elephant jokes, mummy
mummy and submitted jokes. You can

141

even send in your own to be featured on the site.

Gallery of Advertising Parody

http://www.dnai.com/~sharrow/parody.html

Taking a pot-shot at the advertising industry, the Gallery of Advertising Parody invites you to send in parodies of well known tacky adverts. No company is safe from ridicule.

Humour Database *

http://www.humordatabase.com

An excellent searchable database that will assist you in finding a joke for any occasion by topic, age, or popularity. The cheesy ones are always the best!

Monty Python's Flying Circus *

http://www.pythonline.com

An absolute must have. Some people just don't get it do they? Archive of all the best bits, plus information on what the pythons are up to now. A classic site with cracking illustrations.

Loaded

http://www.uploaded.com

"Do not enter this site if you are offended, upset or at all annoyed by swearing, coarseness, nudity, or any other fine British traditions." Well-maintained site from the top lad-mag. Up to date stories, jokes, misfortune and of course rudeness are all available here on tap.

Mark's Brush with Greatness

http://www.geocities.com/Hollywood/Lot/4104/

Quite a humorous site this and packed pull of photos of Mark attempting to rub shoulders with the rich and famous people of the world. George Hamilton, Leonard Nimoy and Bob Dole all make an appearance.

Men Behaving Badly *

http://www.menbehavingbadly.com/

A whole website dedicated to the hit BBC comedy starring Martin Clunes and Neil Morrissey. Learn about the series and the cast. Get to grips with the blokey lingo and join in with a fans forum. Must be viewed whilst drinking lager and dreaming of Kylie!

PAW
http://www.kkcltd.com/paw.html
The Pit of Advertising Wonders celebrates all that is worst about the advertising industry. Enter competitions to create your own spoof headlines and jingles and marvel at other peoples witty or lame duck efforts.

The Stupid Page
http://www.sebourn.com/stupid.html
Dedicated to all things stupid. Read and submit your own stupid stories, jokes and anecdotes.

This Bloke walks into a Bar
http://www.well.com/user/zoodc/bar/index.html
A database of the Worlds greatest jokes starting with "So, this guy walks into a bar.."

The World's Dumbest Crooks
http://www.dumbcrooks.com/
Specialising in burglars, robbers and all other types of felon who make complete fools of themselves in the line of their illegal duties.

Comics

DC Comics
http://www.dccomics.com
The official site for Superman, Batman, and the rest. You can find the latest news and releases, though ordering is from American.

Garfield
http://www.garfield.com/
Full Garfield site covering comic strips, fan club, fun and puzzles. All the usual gang are here. You can even buy stuff from the online catalogue.

Marvel Comics

http://www.marvel.com

Daily news updates feature in this, the home of Spiderman, X-Men, Marvel Heroes and the rest of the mob.

Stan Lee

http://www.stanlee.net

Visit the creator of Spiderman and comic book artist, Stan Lee. Vote for your favourite comic book, and visit the comic book art gallery.

Computing

Amazon Free Fonts

http://www.amazonfonts.com

Unrelated to the bookseller (except by being an affiliate), Amazon offer a large range of free fonts for DTP fans. Be careful what you click on though, this site seems to be affiliated with every online business in the world.

Apple

http://www.apple.com/

Homepage of the famous Mac. Found here are product updates, help forums, system updates and more besides. The i-Mac and g3 feature prominently, as does online purchasing of products.

Dell

http://www.euro.dell.com/

The site of this large supplier of PC's for home and public sector use is well set out, with special offers and technical support. You can make your dream PC here and view the latest kit.

DemoScene

http://www.infuse.org/demoscene/news.php3

If you want to show off your computer, the best way is to use a demo, (a combination of the hottest graphics and the best music). Demos are often artistic masterpieces - download the latest PC ones here!

Essential Guide to Installing Windows 2000

http://www.winmag.com/windows/guides/win2000

If you're having problems with Bill Gate's latest money earning venture, then this site, presented by Winmag.com, will take you through the installation proceedure step-by-step.

Gateway

http://www.gw2k.co.uk

Gateway's site allows you to review their complete range of PCs and peripherals and keep up to date with their latest promotions and special offers. They also provide a step by step guide to buying a PC, and there is an on-line ordering facility.

Help Site

http://help-site.com

Providing online manuals and answers to FAQs for all aspects of computing.

IBM *

http://www.ibm.com

A very large site. Here you can keep abreast of the company's corporate dealings, get help and advice online, take a trip around the entirety of this expansive site with their search engine. You can also buy products.

Junkbusters

http://www.junkbusters.com

A great site for learning to deal with junk email.

Microsoft UK *

http://www.microsoft.com/uk/default.asp

The Microsoft UK site allows you to view the latest releases and information from the computing giants.

Motorola

http://www.mot.com/

Find out what makes your Mac tick, along with a large percentage of the worlds' appliances and robots. Includes information on all products and sponsored events.

Net 4 Nowt

http://www.net4nowt.com

Net 4 Nowt was set up to inform people about the huge range of 'free' ISPs in existance. It provides news on a whole range of UK ISP related issues.

PalmCentral

http://www.handango.com

If you're a Com Palm user then this site has software exclusively for you. Everything is nicely organised and easily searched for.

Register

http://www.theregister.co.uk

UK based IT news from the well-respected journalists at The Register. Updated daily with all of the top stories. Amusing and not without a degree of class, despite the slightly poor design.

Skins 'n' Themes

http://www.skins-n-themes.com

This site is full of graphics to help make your desktop a brighter place. The themes will give Windows 95/98/2000 a new, brighter look, whilst the skins will give Winamp (the MP3 player) a totally different image.

The Matrix

http://www.thematrix.org.uk

If you want to get the Internet cheaper and faster than ever before, you'll need to read The Matrix, which provides UK Internet news on a daily basis.

Tiny Online

http://tinyonline.msn.co.uk

Tiny Online provides not only details of their range of PCs but also has a large amount of general content all powered by MSN.

Dating

Dateline

http://www.dateline.uk.com/

Despite having an ugly site, Dateline have been doing the rounds on the Internet since 1996. They are a pay site, and they do have an annoying way of presenting their clients - but they have a large database, so it must be worth a crack!

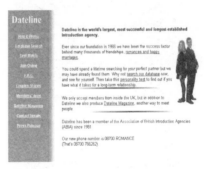

Midsummer Night

http://www.midsummernight.com/

This is another free site, and it's actually quite professional. You can upload your own pictures to go with your profile, and search the database for people living nearby.

Personals 365

http://www.personals365.com

For UK or US users specifically, Personals 365 offers the ability to chat to other users that are online at the same time.

uDate

http://www.udate.co.uk/

Udate have a huge database of members, so your choice is vast. However, despite that, it doesn't seem to allow you to search for people by their location in the country, which is a bit daft. Some long distance liasons could be in order.

UK Personals

http://www.uk-personals.net/

A completely free service which allows you to input your information, upload pictures and search for people by county. A nice site, especially since it doesn't cost anything.

Dictionaries

A Word A Day

http://www.wordsmith.org/awad/index.html

With the use of this site you will increase your vocabulary immensely. You can even sign up to have a word delivered in your email every day. Soon you'll be baffling your friends in polite conversation and will become a genius on Countdown.

Roget's Thesaurus

http://www.thesaurus.com

This inestimable thesaurus can afford to wallow in the scintillating light of it's sublimification, on account of its resplendent search engine. This renders easy the soporific task of employing a literary aid, which was made more encumberant by the incalculable time exhausted by the scrutinization of a standard publication. The splendor of this site is matched only by its transcendence. It does, as the Italians might say, 'volere le mie grasse natiche'.

The Oxford English Dictionary *

http://www.oed.com

The Oxford English Dictionary Online is offering you the chance to help revise one of our greatest traditions. Full history of the publication is on hand, as is a prototype for the new dictionary.

Downloading

. . . .

Acrobat

http://www.adobe.com

Adobe Acrobat files are similar to HTML - they are multimedia pages, which contain text, graphics and sound. Some software provides documentation in Acrobat (.pdf) format, and you can download the free Acrobat reader here.

AVP

http://www.avp.com

AntiVirus Toolkit Pro has proven to be an excellent and regularly updated defence against virii and trojans. There is a time-limited shareware version to download.

Download.com

http://www.download.com

One of the oldest and biggest download sites, Download.com has a massive archive of files. If you're after a piece of shareware, you're very likely to be able to download it here. Gigantic!

Filez

http://www.filez.com/zhub.shtml

Lots of Filez. This once huge search engine has degenerated into a shadow of it's former self - but it could still be useful if you can't find your desired file on Download.com.

FTP Search

http://ftpsearch.lycos.com

Search thousands of FTP sites for the file you need. Particularly useful if you know the filename of your desired file.

Internet Explorer

http://www.microsoft.com/ie

Download Microsoft's Internet Explorer Web browser, complete with Outlook Express.

Netscape

http://www.netscape.com

Netscape's excellent Web browser is also free to download. Get Communicator for an excellent all-round Internet tool.

Norton Antivirus

http://www.norton.com

Can you afford to be without a virus checker? Of course you can't. Norton's is one of the best known.

Shockwave / Flash

http://www.macromedia.com

Some of the greatest browser plugins in the world are available here. Flash and Shockwave allow Websites to provide incredible interactivity and spectacular presentation - without long download times. Download the plugins from this site, then check out the directory of sites which use them.

TuCows

http://www.tucows.com

Big database of software to download. Also a good search engine to help you find software on the Internet. Easy to use.

Winfiles

http://www.winfiles.com

Loads of Windows software to download, including a brilliant section for Drivers. If you're lacking a driver for your 3D card, CD drive or anything else, this is one of the first places you should visit.

Winamp

http://www.winamp.com

An essential download, Winamp allows you to play all of those MP3 sound files

we've been talking about. It's now free to download from this site.

Ecology

BP Amoco *

http://www.bpamoco.com/

A site that as well as promoting itself, has some interesting statistics and articles on world resources, changes in the climate and related subject matter.

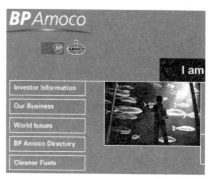

British Trust for Conservation Volunteers

http://btcv.org.uk/

Find out about Britain's largest group of conservation volunteers online. Offer your services, view volunteer and full time vacancies, and shop online to support the organisation.

English Heritage *

http://www.english-heritage.org.uk/

English Heritage's World Wide Web site is

a worthy inclusion here, with a conservation section, new archaeology section, places to visit guide and the excellent National Monuments Record.

Friends Of the Earth

http://www.foe.co.uk/

Top site for earthlings who want to make the most of their planet. Tackles issues ranging from genetically modified foods to renewable energy sources.

Greenpeace *

http://www.greenpeace.org/

Well organised, good looking site which focuses on exactly the right areas of the fight for a better ecosystem. Join online,

take a tour, or keep abreast of up to the minute developments.

Living Almanac Of Disasters

http://disasterium.com/

There is a disaster to cover almost any day in the year. Use this site to find out about what disaster happened on your birthday!

The National Trust *

http://www.nationaltrust.org.uk/

Membership, education, history, information, holidays and more are available on this very well presented site concerned with preserving the British Isles.

The Nature Conservancy

http://www.tnc.org/

A good introductory guide to the world of nature conservation.

Royal Geographical Society

http://www.rgs.org/

Gather information about the society, its literature and any global issues you feel the need to know about. Still a bit underdeveloped but worth a look nonetheless.

United States Environmental Protection Agency *

http://www.epa.gov/

What is America doing to conserve and improve the environment? Your answers are here, from monetary figures through to the levels of pollution in various places.

Volcanoes.com

http://www.volcanoes.com

This site provides a few facts about the volcanoes of the world, but functions mainly as a stepping-stone to other sites. It also tells you how to go about visiting them.

Wastewatch

http://www.wastewatch.org.uk/

Wastewatch is a site set up to promote recycling. It has practical advice on what to do with your rubbish, provides

education packs for schools and a special kids page.

World Wide Fund for Nature *

http://www.panda.org/

This is very good and well-meaning site that enables you to sign petitions against wrong doings the world over. There's plenty here to raise awareness as well as a section devoted to nature artists.

Young People's Trust for the environment

http://www.yptenx.org.uk

A well informed site offering young people (aged between 5 and 16) the opportunity to get involved with conservation and the environment by joining the organisation, attending field trips and organising school seminars.

Employment

Alec

http://www.alec.co.uk/
Alec's free c.v. and jobhunting page
includes links, career advice, and
comprehensive interview skills tips.

Brook Street

http://www.brookstreet.co.uk
Top choice for finding full time and
temporary positions in the office,
secretarial or light industrial areas.

Career Connections

http://www.careerconnections.co.uk/
This site offers career minded people
constructive, alternative solutions to
both finding work and progressing in
their chosen profession.

Give us a Job

http://www.gisajob.com
One of the UK's fastest growing online
recruitment agencies.

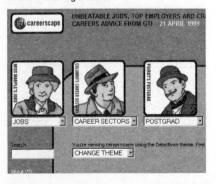

GTI *

http:/www.gti.co.uk
A useful resource for school leavers and
undergraduates who need advice on
career choice, information about job
availability and training.

Hays IT *

http://www.hays-it.com/
Essentially a site that looks for jobs for
you. Give your criteria and hopefully it
will be matched. A good looking site too.

Jobsite

http://www.jobsite.co.uk/
A very slick and well presented site.
Aimed directly at uniting professional
people with jobs and challenging careers
across a broad spectrum of businesses.

Jobs Unlimited *

http://www.jobsunlimited.co.uk
Nicely laid out site allowing you to
search for jobs by sector. There are
recruitement consultancy listings and
and Inernational jobs section.

Extreme Sports

Adventure Time
http://www.adventuretime.com/
This online extreme sports magazine covers a good range of sports and includes reviews of all the new equipment, and a classified section where you can buy and sell your old gear.

ASO
http://www.3rdimension.com/aso/
Good US site devoted to everything inline. Links to bands, newsgroups, product reviews and skating tips. All presented in a straightforward no-nonsense format.

Charged *
http://www.charged.com/
Everything related to extreme sports can be found here. Backyard wrestling, climbing, cycling, fun, 'sin', and action are all covered. A must-see.

Job Net
http://www.netjobs.co.uk
An invaluable site which offers an online database linked to a full compliment of U.K employment agencies and bureaux.

Jobworld *
http://www.jobworld.co.uk/
An excellent job search site which at first looks messy, but is in fact very user friendly.

Stepstone
http://www.stepstone.co.uk
Huge variety of positions grouped within areas of the UK an Europe. As seen on television.

Extremists

http://www.awezome.com/

An extreme sports page covering snowboarding, surfing, motorbikes and mountain biking. The site includes the history of each sport, various pictures and accounts of extreme injuries from around the world.

Injured?

http://aepo-xdv-www.epo.cdc.gov/ wonder/prevguid/

This essential site offers statistical analysis of the type of injuries involved with (aggressive) inline skating, tips on prevention by the use of protective gear, and help on what to do if you are injured.

Inliners *

http://www.inliners.co.uk/

The U.K's leading inline skate manufacturer. Get up to date on the latest products, safety tips and special offers. Find your local dealer and contact other skaters.

Skating

yles, inline skating is the leisure phenomena of ages and all levels of skill.

een captivated by this new sport - the equipment is simple, y on weather conditions or need special surfaces to play on. ntally-friendly form of transit in our overcrowded and joy the great outdoors.

around many years, but inline skates have several advantages rskates have inside and outside wheels, which makes turning contrast, inline skates offer precise and accurate turns akin d many rollerskaters have adopted inline skates for their manoeuvrability.

K2 *

http://www.k2skates.com

The official K2 homepage. These guys want perfection in skating, coupled with unique design. This site offers excellent product information, and a good beginners help section along with the usual tips and tricks.

Knowhere Skateboarding

http://www.knowhere.co.uk/skindex.html

Looking for somewhere to do a 360? Have a look at this site for a guide to the best places in the UK to do just that.

Tum Yeto Digiverse

http://www.tumyeto.com

If you like to move around on small bits of wood with wheels attached to the bottom. This site is where all your skateboarding fantasies can come alive.

Xtreme Scene *

http://www.xtremescene.com/

An extreme sports page that covers

skateboarding, climbing and snowboarding. View photos, find out about contests and enter real life extreme adventures.

Fashion

Ann Summers *
http://www.annsummers.com
Book a party, order a catalogue or try out "virtual lingerie" at this risqué site, home of possibly the best girls' night in.

Burton Menswear
http://burtonmenswear.co.uk/
The high street menswear chain can be found online here. Be it smart, casual or sporting this retail giant has it all.

Clothes Care
http://www.clothes-care.com/
"Welcome to your fashion and clothes care guide". If you need advice on fashion or stain removal, or just want to be a part of a million and one soap powder advertising campaigns, then this is the site for you.

Fashion.Net *
http://www.fashion.net
This well-informed site includes a large online shopping section, world fashion links, news, opinions, chat and much more.

FashionUK
http://www.widemedia.com/fashionuk
A site that dedicates itself to all things fashionable. You are even able to ask

questions about fashion related things on the site.

FashionMall

http://www.fashionmall.com/

A virtual shopping arcade with fashion shops for the gentleman and the lady. There are also related articles and loads of big names are on offer.

Freemans

http://www.freemans.com/

The catalogue fashion specialist now has online fashion and size guides, as well as the option to buy over the Internet.

Gap

http://www.gap.com

Simple site allows purchase of clothes only in America. However there is a UK store locator.

ICompact

http://www.icompact.com

Beauty tips, news and advice. The design isn't fantastic (very pink), but there's plenty to read.

Levi's*

http://www.eu.levi.com

A well designed fashion site where you get to look at clothes on real models and rotate the view from different angles. There is also the option play several mini games.

Pepe Jeans

http://www.pepejeans.com

A very stylist jean site, with arty photos of models wearing their products.

SU214 *

http://www.su214.co.uk/

Excellent online menswear store with all the latest fashions and tips on style.

Swimsuit 2000

http://www.cnnsi.com/features/2000/swimsuit

Lots of girls, in swimsuits. Movies to download, as well as images. Good lord.

Wrangler

http://www.wrangler.com

Wrangler's brand is strongly promoted with the western theme and this site is no exception. Browse the Wrangler catalogue with jeans modelled alongside ten gallon hats. The rest of the range is also represented.

Films

Alfie's Autographs of Hollywood

http://www.alfies.com/

This is a site dedicated to the collection of famous people's autographs and even famous people's addresses. Well worthy.

Ain't It Cool News *

http://www.aint-it-cool-news.com/

This is a site put together by a film fan called Harry Knowles. Apparently a good review by Harry has the potential to affect a film's performance at the box office.

Behind the Scenes

http://library.thinkquest.org/10015/

This is good interactive site that even allows you to create a short movie online. There's also information on what happens behind the scenes when a film is being made, which is interesting for anyone with a passion for the technical side of filmmaking.

British Film Institute

http://www.bfi.org.uk/

Whether you are just a movie fan or actually learning about the medium itself, there is undoubtedly something here for you. Still very much in development but worth a hit.

Celebrity 100

http://www.celebrity1000.com/main.html

Virtual Oscars and Grammy awards rolled into one. Vote online in a whole host of celebrity polls. Use your vote to pander your favourite stars ego.

Disney

http://disney.go.com/disneypictures

Site of the latest and forthcoming films from the company that can keep all ages happy for an hour and a half.

Film 100

http://www.film100.com/

Another means of checking out information on films you know and love as well as hopefully discovering some new ones along the way.

Filmsite

http://www.filmsite.org/

Website that lists the 100 greatest films of all time. Plus another 100 in case they missed any. Also includes sections on Oscar winners and greatest scenes. Plus the top 100 films from other sources to act as a comparison.

Film Unlimited

http://www.filmunlimited.co.uk

A movie site which covers both cinema and video releases. Contains news, reviews, special features and Hollywood gossip.

Film World

http://www.filmworld.co.uk

Movies site which focuses more on arthouse movies rather than the latest main stream movies. Contains a guide to the year's film festivals, cinema listing and the Videoworld, where you can purchase movies on video and DVD.

The Hollywood Reporter*

http://www.hollywoodreporter.com

A place to keep up on any film related gossip and news. TV programmes and music are featured here too.

Internet Movie Database *

http://uk.imdb.com/

Search for material on a film, an actor or a director and check out some reviews.

James Bond Home Page

http://www.jamesbond.com

With a half decent actor back in the role of the world's favourite super spy, the Bond movies will be generating a whole new legion of fans. The wealth of information on these Web pages would appear to be more than up to the challenge.

MGM Studios

http://www.mgm.com

A suitably huge Web site for a suitably huge company. The MGM site has information on past releases as well as films that are currently in production. There is also a shop at the site for you to buy some Bugs Bunny ears!

Normal Guy Movie Reviews

http://www.normalguyreviews.com
Most reviews are written by luvvies or pretentious 'art-critics' - where as Normal Guy Movie Reviews are apparently written by a normal guy. He's probably got two heads and webbed fingers.

Palace: Classic Films

http://www.moderntimes.com/palace/
A fantastic site dedicated to film noir, that most atmospheric and charged of all movie genres. There are many pictures to download onto your system from classics such as Big Sleep and Notorious. On top of this there are lots of well-written features and articles.

Popcorn *

http://www.popcorn.co.uk
A movie site with reviews, hundreds of

pictures, video trailers and audio interviews. The Pop Corn site also contains some cool graphics.

Rough Cut

http://www.roughcut.com/
US Web magazine reviewing the latest video releases, behind the scenes reports and the latest information on forthcoming hits.

Star Wars

http://www.starwars.com
The official site of the blockbuster movies. The site is split into four sections related to each of the four movies with highly detailed information on all the characters, spacecraft, planets, droids, weapons and technology.

The Sync

http://thesync.com
This is a must visit for anyone considering themselves to be a bit of a film buff, as well as anyone who wants to know more about how to broadcast over

the Net.

United International Pictures*
http://www.uip.com/
Have a look at what films are currently in production from this famous Hollywood studio.

Universal Pictures
http://www.mca.com/universal_pictures/
A site that allows you to be right up to speed on movies that aren't even released in this country yet. That will impress your friends won't it?

Urban Legends Reference Page
http://www.snopes.com/movies
The Urban Legends Reference Page tells you about all those little snippets of information that people find so interesting. Like the bit in Star Wars where a Storm Trooper bangs his head.

Virgin
http://www.virgin.net/
Possibly one of the best all round UK

leisure guides. The site includes a cinema finder and lots of up to the minute entertainment news.

Food and Drink

Buitoni*
http://www.buitoni.co.uk/
Quite a good site concentrating on the famous pasta sauce. It links recipes with the places in Italy where they originated, and promotes their full range of food.

Ben and Jerry's
http://www.benjerry.com
Company figures and articles on past, present and future ice cream flavours rub shoulders on this site.

Campbell Soup Company
http://www.campbellsoups.com/
Recipes for making whole meals out of a

single can of soup and how your body will benefit once you've eaten it. Plus all the details on Campbell's range.

Cadbury

http://www.cadbury.co.uk/

Death by chocolate. The definitive site for lovers of chocolate, old or young. Take a tour of the factory, steal some recipes (!), and play to win more chocolate than you could possibly imagine.

Chateau Online

http://www.chateauonline.com

Indulge in the secrets of France's finest wine. The site includes a gift shop, recommended wines and a wine search with parameters including name, varietal, appellation and characteristics.

Cookbooks Online

http://www.cook-books.com/reg.htm

An expansive (some say the largest!) collection of recipes all online. From snacks to dinner parties, you will definitely find what you want here.

Cooking Index

http://www.cookingindex.com

For all things culinary. This site provides some mouth-watering treats and great links. Dieters beware.

Creme Egg

http://www.cremeegg.co.uk

Completely devoted to the chocolate egg, this site contains the same wackiness as the adverts and includes egg related mini games.

Food Network

http://www.foodtv.com/

Lots of recipes and lots of advice for the budding chef are provided by this lively and entertaining site.

Foodwatch *

http://www.foodwatch.com.au/

Sound instruction here on how to eat more healthily. Recipes are provided as well as self-assessment tests to deduce how healthily you are eating at the moment.

Home Farm Foods

http://www.hognet.co.uk/homefarm/

This company offers online ordering of gourmet frozen foods nationwide, with no minimum order or delivery charges and a pay on delivery policy. Delicious.

Ir'n Bru *

http://www.irn-bru.co.uk

"See what Ir'n-Bru can do for you". A really weird site where you can play mad games, view their strange awards, take part in competitions and go orange!

Monsanto

http://www.monsanto.co.uk

Providing the positive argument in the debate about GM foods.

Pillsbury Central*

http://www.pillsbury.com/

This place makes Hagan-Dazs and Green Giant products. As well as recipes there are games and competitions.

The Rare Wine Cellar

http://www.amivin.com

Buy wines from a wide variety of years and regions over the Internet!

Recipes For All Tastes

http://www.mwis.net/~recipeman

A massive selection of recipes, along with hints to help you get more out of your kitchen. Visitors to the site are invited to send in their own recipes.

Spice Guide

http://www.spiceguide.com

All you ever need to know about spices. This site covers their origins, purposes, and which go together the best. There are even recipes you can follow to use your new found knowledge.

The Vegetarian Resource Group

http://www.vrg.org/

No meat from bonkers cows in these recipes, just healthy and nutritious vegetarian grub. There's a newsletter here too.

The Ultimate Directory Of Cooking Sites

Ah ... the Kitchen. The glue which binds families, the foundation of culture, and source of a near endless variety of dishes which - rich or poor - improve the quality of life.

With the Web comes a proliferation of recipe and cooking sites, a virtual library which holds tens of thousands of recipes from across the globe, most of which may be accessed without cost. Our directory is designed to speed you to the exact recipe or cooking information you want; and to give you an idea of what you might expect from the cooking sites we have reviewed.

TUDOCS GRADING

	Just made it.

TuDocs *

http://www.tudocs.com

A site that acts as a database for cooking sites on the net. Reviews of the sites listed are included.

Virgin Cola Chat *

http://www.virgincola.co.uk

Join the "gas room" to chat about almost anything, buy concert tickets on the Virgin ticket hotline, vote on the question of the day and win Virgin goodies.

Football

. . . .

The FIFA Museum Collection

http://www.fifamc.com/

View and even buy some 2000 football related items. Memorabilia, pictures, movies and tours from all over the world are included on this site as well as sporting equipment, toys and much, much more besides.

Football Fantasy League

http://www.fantasyleague.co.uk

The Internet can be used either for actually participating in a fantasy league or merely for gathering all the current statistics. This site offers both.

Football Mastercard

http://www.footballcard.co.uk

Show the strength of your dedication to your football team by applying for a Mastercard bearing their logo. Not every team has one but most do, and you'll be safe in the knowledge that you are helping their cash flow problems.

Football Now

http://www.football.nationwide.co.uk

Not everyone supports Man Utd or Liverpool. Football Now from Nationwide provides football news from all over the UK, but with the focus on the lower leagues.

From the Terrace

http://www.fromtheterrace.co.uk/

This fans-maintained site is a great way to really get into the grass roots of football, and even contribute material yourself. Check out your local club section.

Global Football

http://www.intermark.com/

Keep up to date on the worldwide football scene with Soccer News Online,

163

no matter who you support this site will prove interesting.

MatchFacts
www.matchfacts.com/
Another excellent virtual football universe, also featuring full coverage of the "real world's" week in football.

Pele, Ole
http://www.math.swt.edu/~ec33032/ index.html
A website dedicated to the great man himself. Loads of information on a man whose name should really have been spelt, G-O-D.

Rete!
http://www.soccerage.com
If you want to stay in touch with the European football scene, log on here for news, fixtures and clips from recent matches.

SoccerNet *
http://www.soccernet.com

Up to the minute information on all English and Scottish leagues, the F.A cup and more.

Teamtalk *
http://www.teamtalk.com
Now fully revamped, Teamtalk provides unrivalled news and information on English and Scottish league teams and the UK's national sides.

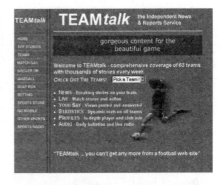

The Football Pages
http://www.ukfootballpages.com
The United Kingdom Football Pages Directory. Find the team you are looking for in this well stocked no-frills database of U.K clubs. A little stripped down, but containing comprehensive content and a user friendly interface.

Upfront
http://www.upfront-online.co.uk/
Well informed website focusing on the struggle for the acceptance of women's football into the mainstream. Match reports, discussion forums, news, links

and feedback make up this comprehensive guide.

Games

The Adrenaline Vault

http://www.adrenalinevault.com
A site for computer game addicts. There's news about the industry as well as the usual wealth of reviews, tips and demos.

Capcom

http://www.capcom.com
The creators of the legendary Street Fighter and Resident Evil series of video games. The site includes links to its Japanese, American and European offices, information on new products, art gallery and an online store.

Games Domain*

http://www.gamesdomain.com
Great site this with plenty of information and interaction.

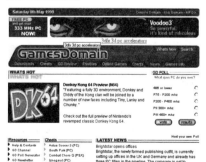

Gamespot *

http://www.gamespot.co.uk/
Very much based around the U.K gaming scene. A very good source of current information that is well presented. You can enter competitions, and view charts and cheats.

Happy Puppy

http://www.happypuppy.com/
Stuck trying to kill that freaky thing in House of the Dead 2? Be stuck no more with the cheats, hints, tips and solutions that this site offers.

Konami

http://www.konami.com/
The official site for the Japanese video game company responsible for the million seller Metal Gear Solid. Includes product information and exclusive insight to their back catalogue of titles.

Pokemon World

http://www.pokemon.com
The website of Nintendo's sensational

165

craze contains the latest Pokemon news and more than enough plugs for related products.

Total Video Games

http://www.totalvideogames.com
A video game site covering Playstation, Nintendo 64 and Dreamcast systems. Includes news, reviews, previews and an extensive range of cheats, player guides and game translations.

Government

10 Downing Street *

http://www.number-10.gov.uk/
Have a look around the home of the Prime Minister at this eye catching site. Lots of in depth politics including the weekly broadcast from the PM. Also some history and biography of past PMs.

British Army

http://www.army.mod.uk/
If you've been tempted to join up by the advertisements on the TV, check this site out for all the information you need.

British Defence Staff

http://www.bdsw.org
This site outlines joint defence initiatives and details of defence relations between the UK and the US. From this site you can examine the British view on policies such as arms control and defence planning.

British Monarchy

http://www.royal.gov.uk
Photos, press releases, and history. For those with an interest in all thing royal this site is fairly basic, but certainly worth investigating. You can find out about the palaces and their visitor information.

Foreign and Commonwealth Office

http://www.fco.gov.uk/
A very informative and current site, providing knowledge in areas such as our relations with other countries and any diplomatic missions that may be underway.

Government Information Service

http://www.open.gov.uk/
Do you want to know exactly what the government is doing for this country as

well as others? A huge site containing mountains of information.

HM Treasury

http://www.hm-treasury.gov.uk/
Not the most exciting site, but if you want to keep on eye on the goings on of the Chancellor, look no further.

Internet Watch Foundation

http://www.internetwatch.org.uk
This site is concerned with the publication of all that is illegal and distasteful on the Internet. There are hotline numbers in case you do stumble across something deemed illegal. The page also defines legal and illegal images for you.

Interpol

http://www.interpol.com
Website for the international police. This site provides a reference library and exhibition providing information on Interpol. Includes press release archives and details of the Worlds' most wanted people.

Local Government Association

http://www.lga.gov.uk/
Providing information on local government issues and details of activities. News and press releases keep the world abreast of those economic regeneration and sex education in school issues.

Metropolitan Police

http://www.met.police.uk
The site for the greater London police force contains news reports, a page of Britain's most wanted, information on recruitment and an in depth history of Scotland Yard.

Nato

http://www.nato.int
The site of the North Atlantic Treaty Organisation allows you to get up to date with the latest happenings from their headquarters. The site provides current mission briefings, press releases, and an online library containing archived official documents and publications.

US versus Microsoft

http://www.usvmicrosoft.com
A regularly updated site which counts down the legal action taken by the US Department of Justice against the computer giant Microsoft.

United Nations

http://www.un.org/
The UN's homepage contains detailed information about all aspects of the United Nations work. This includes details of peacekeeping forces, international law, humanitarian affairs, human rights and international and social developments. The site also allows you to review selected documents and maps and read online publications.

Health and Fitness

3 Fat Chicks on a Diet *
http://www.3fatchicks.com/
Good title for this Website and descriptive of the content. Follow the ups and downs of three dieting ladies to see what they are doing right or wrong.

Food
FOOD REVIEWS New or popular diet foods, updated every Sunday. This week: Lean Cuisine Chicken Medallions with Creamy Cheese Sauce

FAST FOOD INFORMATION Get the skinny on fast food. Detailed nutritional charts for 20 popular fast food restaurants, covering several hundred items!

LOWFAT AND DELICIOUS RECIPES Favorites of ours and our readers, includes complete nutritional data such as fat, fiber, carbohydrates, etc. 36 new recipes added 04/25!

About the girls...
If you'd like to know who we are and why we are doing this, read our bios and journals, then check our progress. Just added: Picture Gallery (please be patient while it loads) if you want to see us before the weight gain, at our heaviest weights, and how we look so far.

Communicate
MESSAGE BOARD Share support, tips, recipes, etc., in a friendly environment of people that share the same concerns, struggles, and successes of weight loss.

CHAT Join your diet buddies in our java chat room

Acupuncture Homepage
http://www.demon.co.uk/acupuncture/index.html
Comprehensive site containing information about the history of the medicine, treatable conditions, research and resources for both patients and practising professionals.

Alcoholics Anonymous
http://www.alcoholics-anonymous.org
Giving information for those addicted to alcohol, with tests to see whether you need their help.

Alternative Medicine Connection
http://www.arxc.com/
An up-to-date site focusing on both the politics and scientific commitment to alternative treatments. Includes an online mail service for patients to exchange help and guidance on what they have found beneficial.

American Heart Association
http://www.justmove.org/
Combat the onset of heart disease by adhering to the advice proffered on this site.

Anxiety
http://www.firststeps.demon.co.uk/
The organisation First Steps To Freedom offers support programmes for those with anxiety disorders.

ASH
http://www.ash.org.uk
As well as being designed to help you give up the dreaded habit, the ASH site also includes helpful advice about suing the tobacco companies of the world and tells you the things the industry does not want you to know.

BeWELL.com *
http://www.bewell.com/
Become and stay both physically and mentally tip top by taking the advice at this site. For men and women.

Today's Health News:

All of today's headlines

Healthy Living electronic magazines

FREE Cancer reports sponsored by

PROCRIT*
EPOETIN ALFA

Search this site

Search   Reset

Exercise and asthma: Garlic: a "hearty" herb

Biorhythms

http://www.facade.com/biorhythm
Get in tune with the planet earth by creating your own personal biorhythm chart. Lifechanging or oddball hokum? You decide.

Blood Transfusion

http://www.blooddonor.org.uk
The home of the U.K blood transfusion service, vital to the health of the nation. Sign up today.

Body, Mind and Modem

http://www.bodymindandmodem.com
If you are interested or even just curious about the martial arts of Aikido and Ki, a force that gives us a strong sense of positivity, have a look around this site. The site also contains exercises and advice.

Boots

http://www.boots.co.uk
Beauty tips and health advice from Britain's leading pharmaceuticals retailer.

The British Stammering Association

http://www.stammer.demon.co.uk
The world over, thousands of people suffer from this impediment to their speech. This Website goes about the task of raising people's awareness of this problem.

CMP Media

http://www.netguide.com/health/
Herbal medicine gets a look in here, along with the latest health related news.

Discovery Health

http://www.discoveryhealth.com
A fascinating, professional medical site from the Discovery team. Lots of info and news, but you might just come away thinking 'Oh god, I've got [insert nasty illness here]'. An excellent site for everyone bar hypocondriacs.

Drkoop.com *

http://doctorkoop.com
An extensive health and fitness site, this allows you to check up on how four people are getting on with their new fitness regime.

E-sthetics
http://www.phudson.com
This takes a look at a hospital for plastic surgery, detailing operations that are available along with a few tasteful photographs.

FDA
http://www.fda.gov
FDA stands for Food and Drug Administration, an organisation who will let you know exactly what's in your drink, your food, and basically anything else you put down your neck.

Fitness Online
http://www.fitnessonline.com
One of the most complete and comprehensive fitness related Web sites around. There are sections where you can shop for fitness goods and ask questions as well as features to watch and read. Very extensive.

FitnessLink *
http://www.fitnesslink.com
As well as providing information on other health and fitness related sites, this site has plenty to offer you on its own.

Go Ask Alice
http://www.goaskalice.columbia.edu
Although this site has a strange name, it is in fact a very accessible site dealing with the personal problems encountered by men and women of all ages. Subjects covered include alcoholism, drug abuse and sexual problems.

Health and Fitness Forum
http://www.worldguide.com/Fitness/hf.html
If you want to achieve a full bill of health this is the site to check out. Advice on various issues including how to maintain a healthy diet and sports medicines are given a down to earth approach.

The Health Site
http://www.bbc.co.uk/health
Another good site from the BBC incorporating detailed sections on health matters, a quiz that determines your life span and a listings database. There is also advice for the medical student and the consumer.

Health Education Authority: Trashed*
http://www.trashed.co.uk
An anti drug site that sets out to inform rather than to preach. Select a drug from either the drugs listed or via the search

engine. Learn about that drug's origins, its effects, how the drug is seen under the law, the composition, and what you should do if you discover someone has taken it.

Healthfinder

http://www.healthfinder.com/

A good starting point for health related Internet searches. Lots of facts are crammed in.

Hypnotica

http://www.bcx.net/hypnosis/

This site is essentially a guide to hypnotising yourself in order to cure yourself of something or improve an aspect of your life.

IFIC *

http://ificinfo.health.org/

Excellent site of the International Food Information Council. With a wealth of information for both the public and educators drawn from comprehensive resources, this is a must-see.

Institute for the Study of Drug Dependence

http://www.isdd.co.uk

A site that takes a more scientific view of drugs. Includes the latest drug related statistics and a library where you can search its database of reports, articles and journals.

Internet Addiction *

http://www.internetaddiction.com

This site takes a light hearted but informative approach to what can be as dangerous to your relationships as many other forms of addiction.

L'Oreal

http://www.loreal.com/

An eye catching site from L'Oreal containing product information and beauty tips.

MedicineNow

http://www.medicinenow.co.uk/

A great site which offers personal, confidential advice and answers on a huge range of medicinal topics. It does involve a small fee, but the professionals involved in the organisation are second to none.

Mediconsult.com

http://www.mediconsult.com/

This is a valuable site offering people with various illnesses the chance to contact someone who can lend a helping hand.

Medisport

http://www.medisport.co.uk/

Using questions to break down the possibilities, this site defines the right procedure and product to aid recovery from injury. There is also a section providing possible preventative measures.

Men's Fitness Online

http://www.mensfitness.com

With so much health and beauty literature around for women it was only a matter of time before men became the

subject matter. Take a visit to this site and get rid of those love handles.

Merck Publications

http://www.merck.com/pubs/

Have a look through the Manual of Diagnosis and see if you've got anything nasty! Much of this site is merely self-promotion, but there is a lot here for medical professionals and curiosity value.

NFSH *

http://www.blonz.com

The Blonz Guide to Nutrition, Food Science and Health. Maintained by Ed Blonz PhD this site concentrates on nutritional ways to improve your health. Many links are included, all of which are personally checked by the man himself.

Nutrition, Food & Health Resources

When Nutrition, Food and Health News Breaks, The Blonz Guide Can Help You Fix It!

Targeting the fields of Nutrition, Foods, Food Science & Health along with excellent search engines and resources for the newbie on up to the ardent webster!

Patient U.K

http://www.patient.co.uk/

Everything you could possibly want as a patient is here. Almost all illnesses are discussed, and extra features include self-help, ethics and complimentary medicine.

Quit Smoking Company *

http://www.quitsmoking.com
It may work for you, it may not, but whatever you get from this site, at least you can say you tried!

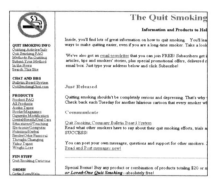

Regaine

http://www.regaine.co.uk
A site for bald men the world over. This Regaine site offers help and advice to the follicly challenged and answers the myth that bald people make better lovers.

Scotland against Drugs

http://www.sad.org.uk
An initiative set up in Scotland to try and prevent children from taking drugs. The site explains its goal and how it intends to tackle the drug problem through educating young people, parents and business.

Summer Skin Care

http://www.icnet.uk/news/sun
This site most importantly informs you how best to prevent skin cancer and also what to check for on your own body. It lets you know who is most at risk and what measures to adopt with regards to your children.

The Truth about Smoking

http://thetruth.com
This very smart site details all of the tactics used by large tobacco companies to ('allegedly') lie to and decieve the public.

Turnstep.com

http://www.turnstep.com/
Without many illustrations to show how its done, it may be a bit difficult learning some of the 4000 routines listed on the Turnstep site. But with such an extensive selection of routines from all over the world, you should find something to suit you.

U.K Healthcare

http://www.healthcentre.org.uk/
The guide to UK medical information on the web. Includes a clinic with resources for patients and carers, resources and forums for healthcare professionals, site of the week and a useful site search facility.

Viagra

http://www.viagra.com

For the bare facts on a product that has already been hyped beyond belief take a long hard look at this Viagra site. It explains what the drug is all about and also what problems may be caused from its use.

Whole Health MD

http://www.WholeHealthMD.com

Ever fancied trying alternative medicines? You may find some interesting info in this well presented site. You even get the opportunity to ask the experts questions.

World Health Online

http://www.who.int

The website from the World Health Organisation provides information about all the latest health issues facing the world today.

Wrecked

http://www.wrecked.co.uk

This site from the Health Education Authority encourages people to think sensibly about alcohol.

Yoga

http://www.timages.com/yoga.htm/

A great personalised yoga routine can be found here. Pictorial representations of all the required positions are on hand along with healthy lifestyle tips.

History

The Ancient Sites Directory *

http://www.henge.demon.co.uk/

An excellent guide to the UK's prehistoric monuments. Offers a searchable text index with links to information, background, location and travel details for all prehistoric sites.

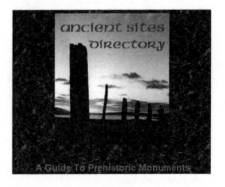

Egyptian Archaeology

http://www.memst.edu/egypt/main.html

Linked to many examples of mummies and artefacts. This site includes full displays from exhibitions and the chance to take a virtual tour of Egypt.

History of the World *

http://www.hyperhistory.com/

A gigantic online reference encyclopaedia, which is presented in an entirely original way. There are important happenings from all over the world and features on the people who have made the world what it is today. Hard to define but simple to navigate.

This webpage shows a sample of the original World History Chart, and links to the award winning project HyperHistory Online, accessible with Netscape 2.0 (or better).

HyperHistory Online is based on the synchronoptic concept and can be regarded as a companion to the World History Chart of Andreas Nothiger. The History Chart can be obtained from here. (An enlarged version of the chart is displayed in many Luxury Hotels around the world as a millennium celebration). Hyper History is growing monthly until the project provides a comprehensive synchronoptic display of world history for the last 3000 years.

The Natural History Museum *
http://www.nhm.ac.uk/
If you don't fancy a trip to the big smoke to see these exhibits in person, this is of course the next best thing. There's a large library of photographs and some great educational stuff. Hey! Learning is fun!

Smithsonian Institution
http://www.si.edu/
An amazingly large collection of artifacts on display at the Smithsonian's Website. This institution has 16 museums in the

US, but you needn't leave dear old Blighty to ogle a fascinating site.

Hobbies andPastimes

Antiques-UK
http://www.antiques-uk.co.uk
A large online resource for antiques collectors including details of dealers and online catalogues with photographs of over 20,000 antiques for sale.

Birdwatch Online
http://www.birdwatch.co.uk
The homepage of Birdwatch magazine containing features, photos and comments from respected twitchers such as Bill Oddie and Steve Rook.

British Gardening Online *
http://www.oxalis.co.uk
This site not only provides plant selectors

and lots of links, but also details of gardens you can visit throughout the UK.

British Horse Society

http://www.bhs.org.uk
Lots of information for the horse lover. The British Horse society's site contains details of riding clubs, diary dates and regularly updated news.

British Walking Federation

http://www.bwf-ivv.org.uk/
This site is packed with information for walks providing, amongst other things, details of trails throughout the UK. If you complete one of their walks you can send off for a cloth badge, how's that for an incentive?

Fishing

http://www.fishing.co.uk
A UK site containing features and plenty of information for the keen angler. All types of fishing are featured including coarse, game and sea. Very detailed.

Gardeners World

http://www.gardenersworld.beeb.com
A superb site. Gardeners World provides masses of information for gardeners. Including plant of the day, a brief weather forecast, news, tips, events diary, gardeners gallery and even the famous gardeners question time.

Lorryspotting

http://www.lorryspotting.com/index.htm
For spotters of Eddie Stobart lorries (no really!). Containing news and pictures of the large fleet of lady lorries and details of how to join the club.

National Cycle Network

http://www.sustrans.org.uk
The National Cycle network opens in June 2000 and will provide 5000 miles of continuous routes throughout the UK. This site will provide you with all the info.

Ramblers Association

http://www.ramblers.org.uk/
The Ramblers association is at the forefront of campaigns to keep and maintain public footpaths and give ramblers the right to roam. The site is well laid out with details of trails, events, campaigns, publications and how to join.

Royal Mail Stamps

http://www.royalmail.co.uk/athome/stamps

The Royal Mail's provides Philatelic services provide details of the latest stamp releases and upcoming stamp related events. If ever a site had First Edition written all over it.

Royal Mint

http://www.royalmint.com

A good looking site with all the latest coin related news as well as competitions and coin talk.

All material copyright Royal Mint 2000. Site last updated February 10 2000. Site maintained by *The British Royal Mint*

Trainspotting

http://www.lexcie.zetnet.co.uk/modular/mh-trains.htm

Not the cult film with Ewan Macgregor but the real deal. Shunters, locos tube stock and much more, with photos. Notebooks at the ready then.

Wine Mine

http://www.winemine.com

Plenty of useful tips and information for wine makers to read and share. Something to mull over during the long winter nights.

Kids

Animal Information Database

http://www.seaworld.org

One of the best nature sites on the Internet, this page is run by the American SeaWorld organisation. Watch feeding and fun with all animals, not just water dwellers. Play games and test your wildlife knowledge.

ArgoSphere

http://www.argosphere.net/

A site to keep the youngsters at bay for a while. Loads of games and quizzes all divided into specific sections. A great resource.

ASfAA

http://www.marlo.com/

The Awesome Site for All Ages. Aged 15-95? Then there's something here for you. Read cartoons, illustrated stories and stockpile some jokes, or simply have fun!

Barney Online

http://www.barneyonline.com/

Probably aimed at slightly younger children, this is an educational as well as fun site packed with animation from the loveable pink dinosaur. Still you don't have to be young to appreciate Barney!

Blue Peter *
http://www.bbc.co.uk/bluepeter
Remember the glory days of John Noakes
and Shep? Explore the archive of
presenters old and new and amuse the
children for a few hours.

Children' Television Workshop
http://www.ctw.org
Get the lowdown on Oscar the grouch,
Big Bird and Elmo with this excellent
interactive learning site. All modes of
pre-school education are covered very
well here, from shapes to memory,
numbers to the alphabet.

Colouring In *
http://coloring.com
A great interactivity site for children,
allowing them to choose ready-drawn
pictures to colour in, in real-time.

Crayola
http://www.crayola.com
Some artistic tools for children to enjoy
and learn from. There's some games
thrown in there too.

CyberPlagrounds
http://www.freenet.hamilton.on.ca/~aa937
This expansive resource features links for
children of all ages. Topics covered
include science, music, computers,
animals, sports, art and more.

Cyberteens
http://www.cyberteens.com
The aim of this site is to promote
creativity and allow kids the world
over the opportunity to voice their
opinions or ask questions on any topic
they like.

The Disney Channel
http://www.disneychannel.co.uk
A Web site companion to the satellite
station. Provides a TV guide to the
station as well as information on the
presenters. Plan those classic movie
watching times.

Disney Online

http://www.disney.co.uk

Check out clips, cartoons and plenty of animations with the companion site to Disney's satellite channel and EuroDisney.

Dr Seuss' Seussville *

http://www.seussville.com

The Cat in the Hat is back on your laptop! Fun games to play on this site which features all Dr Seuss' brilliant characters. It looks fantastic too.

Enid Blyton

http://www.blytonweb.co.uk

For the younger children this site offers the chance watch cartoons and play with Noddy and his old mate Big Ears. Includes a history of all Enid Blyton's books.

Fox Kids

http://www.foxkids.com

The popular children's channel website (and home of Woody Woodpecker). Play games, see what's new and join in the activities of the Fox Kids Club.

Foxy Online

http://www.tumyeto.com/tydu/foxy/ foxy.html

If you are teenage and female looking for something to do, check out the site at Foxy Online. There are people to speak to if you need help, and also horoscopes.

Goosebumps

http://place.scholastic.com/ goosebumps/index.htm

The huge success of R L Stine's Goosebumps books have resulted in various spin off TV series. This Website is a companion to both the books and the show, with a bit of a biography on the author and creator.

Hello Kitty's Tea Party

http://www.groovygames.com/kitty/

Another educational site, this time for slightly younger kids. Loads of pictures and games with plenty of interaction.

Homework High

http://www.homeworkhigh.co.uk

A fun educational site from Channel 4, which does live afternoon and evening learning sessions. Covers English, Maths, History and more!

How Stuff Works*

http://www.howstuffworks.com

Although primarily for children, this site

has enough to entertain the adults as well. How do planes fly? How do fridges keep cold when the back of them is so hot? Answers to all these and more.

I Spy

http://www.geocities.com/~spanoudi/spy
Keep the very young engaged with this very simple version of the guessing game.

The Junction

http://www.the-junction.com
A teenage magazine from those people at Virgin. There's places you can chat to other like minded beings, and you can also listen to music, play games or check out the latest gossip

Kids Publishing

http://www.kidpub.org/kidpub
KidPub is an essential resource for all budding young writers providing a forum for the publication of children's stories from around the globe.

KidsZone *

http://freezone.com
A good site for kids who want to feel grown-up. Comics, games, web page tools and a great chat area.

Kidsurfer

http://www.child.net/forkids.htm
Very comprehensive kids' site giving information on other sites they may well enjoy. There are opinions to give and prizes to win.

Lego

http://www.lego.com
Welcome to the world of Lego. Get the net lowdown on all Lego products, plus information on the great theme parks and forthcoming events. Easy to use and fun for all ages.

Letsfindout.com

http://www.letsfindout.com/
A very nice looking American website which will satisfy the appetite of even

the most information hungry youngster.

Little Bo-Peep

http://www.megabrands.com
Tots will love these very popular stories, and they can click on any word for pronunciation. Be warned, the music at this site is a bit grating however!

Mania

http://www.mania.com
Pure multi-media heaven can be experienced at this site, where there is information on games, TV shows, movies and even toys. The toys can be purchased online.

Mr Potato Head *

http://www.mrpotatohead.com/
Find out more about everybody's favourite spud. Highlights include the Tater Timeline, games for big and little kids and the chance to see the latest Mr Potato Head toys.

Puffin UK

http://www.puffin.co.uk
A site devoted to the off shoot of Penguin. Meet the author of the month and check out any related TV and video releases.

Reach Out

http://www.reachout.asn.au/
This site is somewhere for depressed and even suicidal teenagers to go for help. There are many services available here to guide both the teenager and the worried parent.

React

http://www.react.com/
This one is primarily designed for teenagers. Subjects covered include articles on what might be considered an average body weight. Teens can chat to each other as well via e-mail.

Scalextric

http://www.scalextric.co.uk/
The website of one of the coolest toys ever produced. From here you can find your nearest UK stockists, see new products and join the Scalextric club.

Shout Magazine

http://www.dcthomson.co.uk/mags/shout
As you would expect from a teenage girls magazine there are horoscopes, fashion and beauty items and articles about health and fitness.

Stone Soup *

http://www.stonesoup.com/

An Electronic Magazine written and illustrated by children aged 8 to 13. Over ten thousand pieces are received every year, and the emphasis is purely on the creativity of young people.

Techno Teen Advice

http://www.technoteen.com/advice/

A Web site offering help and advice run by teenagers for teenagers. It is both intelligent and extensive in its subject matter.

Teddy Bear Search Engine

http://www.teddybearsearch.com

Collect Teddy bears? Then use this search engine to find exactly what you're looking for. It has a large directory of sites in it's database, and even covers beanies!

Teen Challenge WorldWide Network

http://www.teenchallenge.com/

This site aims to help "the transformation of restored individuals into useful, productive, law-abiding citizens".

Teletubbies

http://www.bbc.co.uk/education/ teletubbies/

This is another new site from the BBC and if you're a fan there is everything here you could wish for. It really will keep your tot, (and yourself?), amused for a long time.

Theodore Tug Boat

http://www.cochran.com/theodore/

Theodore Tug Boat is a Canadian cartoon and this is a multimedia version. Great if your child is just learning to read with episodes to entertain along with an interactive story.

Thomas the Tank Engine

http://www.thomasthetankengine.com

A good educational site with a lot of games to play. The site is much more beneficial under adult supervision.

Warner Bros. Online

http://www.warnerbros.com

A very big site as you'd imagine, and one with a broad range of things to see and do. Movies, cartoons, TV and comics take up the space in this well produced offering.

Yahooligans *

Http://www.yahooligans.com/

The ever-popular search engine in a

children-friendly guise. Basically as powerful as the main search engine, it has all "dubious" content removed, and kid-specific site pointers.

Language

AltaVista Translator
http://babelfish.altavista.digital.com/ cgi-bin/translate?
A good simple converter of Spanish, Italian, German and French text into English. Still not one for Glaswegian or Cockney then?

Esperanto World
http://www.webcom.com/~donh/ esperanto.html/
The most successful 'created' language has many good links and news stories here, as well as help and news groups, and a good introduction to the language as a whole.

H.E.L
http://ebbs.english.vt.edu/hel/hel.html/
The History of the English Language. This site has everything you need to know concerning our language from Norse runes to Middle English right up to modern dialects.

Internet Press
http://gallery.uunet.be/internetpress/ diction.htm
Perhaps the best place to start looking for those language related sites. This provides information on other online services such as translators and many different types of dictionaries. No pictures but extremely useful.

Klingon
http://www.kli.org/
The Klingon Language Institute. A must have for any devoted Star Trek fan. Here you can gather information on the language and "culture" of the Klingon people and learn to communicate with other Trekkies.

Merriam-Webster
http://www.m-w.com/
This well established publisher takes its first steps on to the Net with this huge and comprehensive dictionary of words, phrases, abbreviations and, quite literally, a lot more.

Magazines

Cosmopolitan

http://www.cosmopolitan.com
There is lots of information on this site. Features include a rough guide to the Internet, skin care information and regular articles on celebrities.

Empire

http://www.empireonline.co.uk
The site of the movie magazine. Regularly updated with news, reviews and previews of the latest mainstream movies.

FHM

http://www.fhm.cm
Website of the UK's most popular lifestyle mag for men. Includes features, jokes, hosts of pretty women and an on-line shop selling books, holidays and clothing. Plus a chance to appear in the mag yourself.

Handbag.com *

http://www.handbag.com
Aimed squarely at female surfers, Handbag is a large site providing features, chat, jobs information, horoscopes, listings, shopping and much more. Everything is well presented, if slightly on the pink side.

Loaded

http://www.uploaded.com/
"Do not enter this site if you are offended, upset or at all annoyed by swearing, coarseness, nudity, or any other fine British traditions." Well maintained site from the top lad-mag. Up to date stories, jokes misfortune and of course rudeness are all available here on tap.

National Geographic *

http://www.nationalgeographic.com/
This magazine site is principally focussed on the USA, but it's excellently put together with a fine selection of old articles to look at.

NewsRack

http://www.newsrack.com/

This site narrows down your magazine search by first offering you a globe. Click on a continent, click on a country and then decide what magazine or newspaper you wish to look at. Simple or what?.

Ooze

http://www.ooze.com

Website of rather bizarre magazine which sets out to insult anybody and everybody by parodying popular genre magazines. Not for the easily offended.

Private Eye *

http://www.private-eye.co.uk/

Might not be worth a visit if you subscribe to this magazine, purely because this site echoes it. Still, there's some very witty and sardonic satire here including the popular St. Albion parish newsletter

Rolling Stone *

http://www.rollingstone.com

Cult music magazine with music news, videos, radio, and articles for fans of the US music scene.

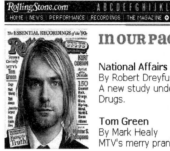

Scene One *

http://www.sceneone.co.uk

UK entertainment guide, listing all that's happening in the world of cinema, gigs, comedy and live theatre. Plus details of new music, books and video.

Suck Daily

http://www.suck.com

Online magazine taking a quirky look at

America and beyond. With a bit of everything thrown in.

Ziff Davis

http://www8.zdnet.com

The site to come to for hundreds of reviews of PCs, peripherals and software. A truely awsome resource if you need some advice.

Music

A&R

http://www.taxi.com

If you want to get ahead in the industry then TAXI could be the resource for you, offering online consultancy from Artists and Recordings people. You have been warned.

Addicted to noise

http://www.addict.com

As its name suggests, this site is devoted to the love of heavy music, namely rock and industrial. News and reviews are available online as well as forums and discussions.

All-Music Guide

http://www.allmusic.com

A big site with an unflounderable search engine. Read brief accounts of musicians' life stories, and more importantly see what records they've released and

whether or not they're still available. An American site, but UK bands and performers are in there too.

BURBS

http:www.burbs.org.uk/

Truly huge site devoted to the profiling of unsigned British rock bands. Hundreds of artists feature here, with biogs and samples of songs available. A must see site.

Buying Music

http://www.tunes.com/

An excellent online record shop that not only offers reviews but also allows you to set up a personal profile and then give recommendations based on your tastes in music.

Catatonia

http://www.catatonia.net/

The very sparse website of the slightly outspoken and very Welsh band. Find out the latest news and tour information and buy merchandise online.

Circa

http://www.circa99.freeserve.co.uk

Minimalist new site from the band being heralded as the new Radiohead. Find out what makes the guys tick, the colour and bands of the month, and send in your favourite recipes. (and yes.. the drummer works for FKB Publishing).

Classical

http://www.musdoc.com/classical/
For those with a passion for classical music they can find everything on this site from concerts, to new pieces, to reviews. There is even the option to enter into discussions.

Classic FM

http://www.classicfm.co.uk/
The Net companion for the magazine and radio station maintains its aims for making the world of classical music approachable for everyone, not just the select few experts. A good, well presented site.

Classical Net

http://www.classical.net/
An independent site, but an extremely good one all the same. Loads of articles and biographies on the composers and a guide on how best to begin a classical music collection. A superb effort.

Dance Music

http://www.juno.co.uk/
This site deals exclusively with contemporary dance music, be it house, techno, underground or gabba. Reviews of current and forthcoming tracks are included, along with comprehensive radio and resource links.

Dot Music

http://www.dotmusic.com

A music site which covers news and reviews of the latest pop music. Includes the top 40 UK charts, previews of new songs, interviews and an online shop where you can purchase discounted CDs, albums, singles, vinyl records and music videos.

Drum 'N' Bass Arena *

http://www.breakbeat.co.uk/
An intelligent site aimed at the discerning Drum N Bass enthusiast. Take a trip to the site to read interviews of the genres leading lights, news and also reviews. If your tastes lie with Celine Dion and Genesis, avoid it.

Elevator Music

http://www.midifarm.com/
This page allows you to download a multitude of hits from television, the stage, the charts and more, all in synthesised MIDI format. Bliss.

Elvis Presley *

http://www.mgm.com/elvis/

The MGM site devoted to the king of rock and roll. Visit the Elvis shrine, purchase exclusive gift packages online and even ask a virtual Elvis for advice.

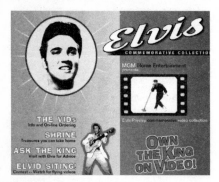

Gramophone

http://www.gramophone.co.uk

A classical and jazz site from the makers of the magazine of the same name. There's 24,000 reviews from the past 15 years worth of issues along with selected articles and features.

Gigs

http://www.giglist.com

Keep up to date with all elements of live music in this country with this well-informed gig listing. Find out who's playing where, get up to date on industry news, reviews and ads, and even buy CD's online.

Live Music

http://www.liveconcerts.com

A great way to catch your favourite bands at their best (live!). This resource offers extensive archiving of live events. Find out where your favourite band has played in the past.

Motown *

http://www.motown.com

A site devoted to the world's most famous record company. Read about the label's history and learn about classic Motown performances.

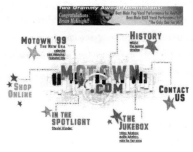

MTV Online

http://www.mtv.com

Aimed entirely at a mainstream American Web audience. Don't expect to be stimulated if you're into the alternative scene in a big way.

Music365

http://www.music365.co.uk

More mainstream than a lot of sites of this nature, this is a very attractive and current site.

Netaid

http://www.netaid.org

A Website set up to promote development and alleviate extreme poverty across the world. The site was launched with a massive online concert including the likes of Robbie Williams, Bono and Eurythmics. The site allows you to view star profiles and brief histories of the artists, as well as donate money.

NME

http://www.nme.com/
Love it or hate it, NME has held its place at the top of the British music paper scene for its entire history. Still essential for upcoming tour dates and a good laugh to boot!

Sun Records

http://www.sunrecords.com
The recording company for artists such as Patsy Cline, Roger Miller and The Vogues. Find out more about their artists, purchase albums and clothes online and play sun related games on a slot machine.

The Ultimate Band List *

http://www.ubl.com/
If you've got a cool band name you don't want other bands to nick, register it here. Similarly, check the name you've got doesn't already exist.

Woodstock

http://www.woodstock69.com
A tribute site to the fabled 60's hippy concert. Contains stories and photos if you need reminding what it was like.

Nature and Pets

Endangered Species

http://www.eelink.net/EndSpp/
Well featured resource site giving information on regions containing endangered species. The site also outlines the work being done by many different organisations to help protect wildlife and comprehensive lists of extinct animals.

Entomology *

http://www.ent.iastate.edu/imagegallery
A wide range of images and photographs are collated here for insect fanatics. The high quality of the posted shots makes this site a must see for any biologist.

Green cloverworm

Green cloverworm.

Gardenworld

http://www.gardenworld.co.uk/

The ultimate resource for the budding horticulturist. Here you will find a detailed database of garden centres and suppliers across the UK, as well as online shopping, a gardeners diary and garden answers.

Inter-Species Telepathy

http://www.CyberArk.com/animal/ telepath.htm

Spooky site documenting telepathic experiences of pet owners with their beloved animals. There are some uncanny instances documented, along with links to other material evidence and discussion groups.

Nature Collection *

http://www.secondnature.com/ nature.htm

Lavish site featuring artwork from many amazing wildlife artists. Montages of images are available to view and add to your screensaver. The wonderfully

presented pictures are eye candy of the highest order.

Alaska Wilderness by Art Wolfe

Art Wolfe, internationally celebrated nature photographer, presents an exciting adventure into Alaska's wilderness. Included are breath-taking views of snow covered Mt. McKinley reflections on Wonder Lake, a bright rainbow above the lush Canning River valley, sunset over Alsek Glacier, and a bull moose peering above a field of wildflowers in Denali National Park.

Horses in the Spotlight by Ron Kimball

Ron Kimball, award-winning and frequently published horse photographer, presents an exciting spectrum of horses including the Clydsdale, Arabian, Belgian, and Lippizan. Collection includes a herd of wild horses galloping through the snow, horses dodging a wrangler's lasso, two brown foals nuzzling each other, a black stallion enjoying the surf, and more dramatic scenes.

Mothers and Babies by Art Wolfe

World class nature photographer Art Wolfe captures the fascinating world of mother and baby creatures. With warmth and candor, Wolfe photographs numerous animal families including river otter, hippopotamus, gorilla, wolf, bald eagle, bison, harbor seal, and wood stork. His unique animal photographs have been published worldwide.

NetFysh

http://www.netfysh.com

Buy small, easy to care for underwater pets such as Sea Monkeys and Triops! A gaudy site, but functional and you can order online.

Pet Place

http://www.ddc.com/petplace

All of your favourite household friends are featured here, including dogs, cats and reptiles. Submit a pets' information for inclusion on the site and read about pet rescue operations and care techniques.

Virtual Cats and Dogs

http://www.virtualkitty.com/

Cool site which allows you to adopt a "virtual" cat or dog, contact other "pet owners", suggest toys and basically have a bit of fun.

You Grow Girl!

http://www.yougrowgirl.com

Despite having what is possibly the worst name imaginable, You Grow Girl offers plenty of fascinating tips and tricks for the lady gardener. Probably more suitable to young ladies.

News

BBC News 24

http://news.bbc.co.uk/

In most web users eyes, this is 'the' online news site. Clear and unbiased views are well presented, with regular updates and interviews with newsmakers of the moment.

CNN

http://www.cnn.com/

Up to the minute breaking stories form around the globe with America's Atlanta based news giant. From war to cookery, you'll find it here with regular updates.

Evening Standard *

http://www.thisislondon.co.uk/

The online edition of London's ever-popular rag, the city's top stories are all here as well as the what's on guide, horoscopes and more.

Guardian Unlimited *

http://www.guardian.co.uk/

Most of the news articles that go to making up The Observer and its weekday counterpart The Guardian are available at this extensive site.

Internetnews.com

http://www.internetnews.com/

A site divided into areas including stock prices and business. Also Provides Internet information as well as news.

ITN Online

http://www.itn.co.uk

This ITN news site offers sound news coverage the world over with regular updates amd analysis.

News Index

http://www.newsindex.com

A cool way to find most top international stories. Here you can search a host of publications and online news outlets worldwide.

NewsNow

http://www.newsnow.co.uk

Whether its news on the arts, business matters, sport or whatever, there is a news page here for you.

Private-Eye *

http://www.private-eye.co.uk

Not really news as such, but a refreshing, satirical look at the latest developments in affairs both national and international.

The Chronicle

http://www.chronicleworld.org

The UK's first internet news magazine focusing on the affairs of black communities. The site features up to date news as well as community projects and news forums.

The Onion

http://www.theonion.com

A spoof American newspaper providing funny bogus news stories.

The Telegraph

http://www.telegarph.co.uk

The Electronic Daily Telegraph offers in-depth home news and top stories with plenty of pictures and background information. Good stop for a daily roundup of headlines.

The Times/ Sunday Times

http://www.the-times.co.uk/ or
http://www.Sunday-times.co.uk/

Save money and paperboy's backs with the times online. Offers the entirety of both papers at the push of a button. Truly a modern publishing breakthrough.

Online Gaming

Gamefan Network

http://www.gamefan-network.com

Providing news, reviews and links for the online gaming community.

Gameplay Community

http://www.gameplay.com/community

The home of Wireplay, the online gaming community. Find out all the happenings in the clubs and leagues and read the latest online gaming news.

Gamespy

http://www.gamespy.com

Similar to Wireplay, Gamespy is a small piece of software that pings hundreds of games servers to see who's playing where. As well as being able to download Gamespy, the site has gaming news and upgrades.

Halflife.org

http://www.halflife.org

This is the ultimate site for Halflifers. News, reviews, interviews, patches, and a whole series of hosted sites (including clan sites). A brilliant site for Half Life / HL Team Fortress fans everywhere.

Leisure District

http://www.leisuredistrict.net

Fancy skiving off work? Then do so, with the aid of Leisure District. Lots of very odd games and other very strange diversions. Pointless and stupid, but it might help you waste a few hours.

MSN Gaming Zone

http://www.zone.com

The Zone is the online gaming site from Microsoft. It contains news, links, events, a shop, downloads and more for hundreds of games.

On-Line

http://www.on-line.co.uk

Up and coming developer of On-Line games, including Auto-Mayhem, Art of Kings and Iron Wolves.

Online Gaming League

http://www.ogl.org

Maintained by volunteers, The Online Gaming League provides ladders leagues and tournaments for the most popular online games.

Online Gaming Library

http://www.oglibrary.com

The Online Gaming Library links to servers and gives online gamers the chance to post and read the latest online gaming news. A little on the dull side.

Planet Quake

http://www.planetquake.com
One of the definitive Quake sites, Planet Quake is a must-visit for anyone that plays any version of Quake online. Seriously.

Planet Quake III Arena

http://www.planetq3.com
Quake III is playing second fiddle to Half Life, but it's still one of the most popular multiplayer games of all time. This site contains everything from skins and patches to screenshots, movies, news and gossip!

Sega Dreamcast

http://www.sega-europe.com
Since the UK launch of Dreamcast there have been promises of online gaming facilities. Get the latest news on how and when this is expected at Sega's European home.

Tribes: Planet Starsiege

http://www.planetstarsiege.com
This is a top site for fans of the jetpacking multiplayer experience that is Tribes. Graphically it's not too hot, but there's loads of news and downloads - including piles of Mods and scripts.

Unreal Tournament Center

http://www.utcenter.com
Unreal was a bit of a flop online until Unreal Tournament was released. This new improved multiplayer game took audiences by storm. This is probably the best site, with all of the usual news and downloads.

Who Wants to be a Millionaire?

http://homepages.tesco.net/~thedoodiest /wwtbamu/index.htm
Oh, it's easy to give the answers sitting at home on your armchair. But can you do it yourself? This Internet based challenge will help you to find out. You can't win anything and it's a bit crude, but it's entertaining for a few minutes of fun.

World Opponent Network

http://uk.won.net
The power behind online gaming. The network links hundreds of servers together, which means that any time, day ot night, you will always find somebody to shoot at. The site includes all the latest downloads and patches.

Yahoo Games

http://www.yahoo.com
Yahoo offer several games to members,

including card games and old-style arcadey types.

Parenting

Babycare Corner

http://familyinternet.com/babycare
This site takes a mature approach to answering your Frequently Asked Questions about baby health, growth, injuries, problems, and behavioural issues.

FI Parenting Sites
Pregnancy Place
Planning for a family and products for Mom,Dad, and Baby

Babyhood

http://www.babyhood.com
Babyhood's Homepage. This page focuses on infants from birth to roughly 24 months. It includes baby homepages, childcare, health and safety issues, recreation and early reading techniques.

Babyworld

http://www.babyworld.co.uk
Well presented site offering information

on all aspects of babies, from pregnancy to feeding. Many related links are available, including toys, competitions, and a baby search engine.

UK Parents

http://www.ukparents.co.uk
A light and airy monthly ezine for UK Mums and UK Dads. Within the site you will find news, features, competitions and forums.

Pop Culture

A1

http://www.a1-online.com
Brighter than bright boyband A1 have a large following, and this is reflected in their online presence. This is the official site, so don't expect much gossip, but it does have lots of very nice Macromedia Flash material, which adds to the overall experience with sound and interactivity.

All Saints

http://pluto.spaceports.com/~quixoft/alls aints.html
This fairly attractive site contains a lot of great stuff, including interviews, pictures and video clips. It's one of the best All Saints sites we've found on our travels!

B*wiched *

http://www.b-witched.com

The official site of the denim clad Irish girlie band. Find out more about the girls, listen to their singles and join the B*witched mailing list.

Boyzone *

http://www.boyzone.co.uk

The official site of Ireland's number one boy band. The site is split into five main categories, The Newz for all the up to the minute gossip, The Boyz where all the members profiles can be found, The Zone for competitions and chat, The Gigz to find out where they are performing and The Tunz for new releases and discography.

Britney Spears

http://www.britneyspears.org

Teenage pop sensation Britney has plenty of fan sites, but this is one of the best. Brilliantly designed with lots of content. Aguilera got the Grammy though..

Buffy the Vampire Slayer *

http://www.buffy.com

The official site of the cult TV hit. Chat with other fans, visit the mortuary to see plotlines of past episodes, play the interactive game and much more.

Christina Aguilera

http://www.christina-aguilera.co.uk

Another blonde teenage pop sensation, Christina Aguilera has followed in the footsteps of her ex-pal Britney. This site is very presentable, and has video and pictures to download. You can also read about her latest UK TV appearances.

Eddie Izzard

http://www.izzard.com

The official site of everybody's favourite

transvestite comedian.

Mr Showbiz

http://mrshowbiz.go.com
A US site providing up to the minute celebrity gossip.

Leonardo Dicaprio

http://www.dicaprio.com
The blonde star that women swoon over is a popular subject for soppy Websites. This is one of the better ones because it exercises a modicum of restraint and is nice to look at. Staggeringly, it's had five million hits in the past five years. Brilliant.

MTV

http://www.mtv.com
Despite having been around for ages, MTV refuses to become unfashionable. Their Website is packed to the gills with various information and news. It's easy to navigate, and more than just a cheap advert for the TV station. Recommended.

Oasis

http://www.geocities.com/SunsetStrip/Alley/2254/index.html
Oasis Webmasters had a fight on their hands a couple of years ago, after Sony threw a strop - but now they're back and better than ever. This site has dozens of pages, covering bootlegs, awards, tour-dates, news, and just about everything else you could ever want. Remarkably, it's still being kept up to date.

S Club 7

http://www.sclub.com
S Club 7 come to you from the same producer as the Spice Girls - only the girls in S Club 7 are far more attractive. Well.. all but one. As expected, most SC7 sites are owned by younger fans, but this official site is brilliant. Really flashy and with loads of behind-the-scenes information. Excellent!

Spice Girls

http://superspice.hypermart.net
Most Spice Girls sites are very poor indeed, so it's surprising to see one which is even half decent. This is a fairly nice site which is somewhat out of date, but brimming over with information. There are more than enough links on here to get you up to date on Spicey matters.

VH1

http://www.vh1.com
The VH1 site is very nicely designed. A

lot of work is constantly going on with this site, but the navigation is made slightly more difficult as a result. Still an excellent site.

Westlife
http://www.geocities.com/aiko_westlife/westlife.htm
Don't be fooled by the awful layout of this site. It's absolutely full of Westlife pictures, articles, links, polls and information. Worth a look.

Property
....

Find A Property *
http://www.findaproperty.com
A site that is always up to date and easy to understand that covers the property minefield that is the south west of London.

GA Property Services
http://www.gaproperty.co.uk

Allows you to search for a selection of properties from GA Property's complete UK database.

Home Hunter
http://www.homehunter.co.uk/
If you're looking to buy a new pad or looking to sell your old one, you could do worse than to check here first. This is a site that deals with the buying and selling of property all over the UK.

Pro Net – Property Highway
http://www.pro-net.co.uk
This site incorporates all the better property Web sites and pools them into one huge database. The information is broken down into estate agents, locations, prices and property types. A good place to start looking for property.

Today's Homeowner
http://www.todayshomeowner.com/
Need some help erecting that fence? Fancy a makeover of your home? If so, visit this site and suffer no more in DIY hell.

UK Property Gold
http://www.ukpg.co.uk
Placing an advertisement at this site costs absolutely nothing and is therefore ideal if you are looking to sell your home. As well as scoring a huge hit rating, you can have a picture of your property online.

UpMyStreet *

http://www.upmystreet.com/
Comprehensive is the word that applies
to this great site. Find out about the
suitability and features of any place in
the UK including schools, employment
and house prices. An ideal resource if
you're thinking of moving to a new area.

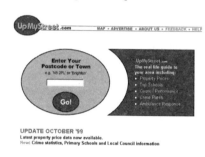

UPDATE OCTOBER '99
Latest property price data now available.
New: Crime statistics, Primary Schools and Local Council information

Psychic

Castle Of Spirits

http://www.castleofspirits.com
Check out some fictional and non-
fictional ghost stories and scare yourself
to death! There are some great stories
here, but feel free to submit your own.

Horoscopes 4U

http://www.horoscopes4u.com
Find out what the future holds in store.
Enter your personal details to receive a
free chart.

Nessie on the Net

http://www.lochness.co.uk
Scotland's first official Nessie web site.
Contains a Loch Ness web camera, so you
can search for the mythical beast from
the comfort of your own home.

Pandora's Box

http://www.pandbox.com
Take a trip to Pandora's Box, a virtual
coffee bar. Read poetry and have your
tarot cards read. Plus more besides.

Reincarnation History

*http://www.best.com/~dna/don/CaseHist
ory.html/*
This well-read site offers actual evidence
of an individual's regression performed by
Don Showen in 1976. Really believable
and spooky, this is a fine example of the
technique.

Russell Grant

http://www.russellgrant.com
The cuddly stargazer provides weekly and
yearly horoscopes and on-line tarot
readings plus quiz games, messageboard
and a biography of the man himself.

Schloss Reichenstein *

http://www.caltim.com/reichenstein/
Find out about Germany's infamous Baron
without a head who lives on the river
Rhine. A guided tour, history of the
castle and even holiday plans are all
here.

Sci-Fi Net

http://www.sci-fi-net.com/

All you sci-fi fans out there can now obtain your memorabilia on line. Get hold of videos and books via this site, on programmes such as The X-Files and Dr. Who. Break downs on specific episodes are available too.

SuperScope

http://www.superscope.com

Receive easy to understand online readings from this slightly simple site.

Tarot

http://www.talisman.net/tarot/

A whole host of tarot card related information can be accessed here, from normal readings to specialist sessions, even using an ordinary pack of cards to predict the future.

Uri Geller's Psychic City

http://www.urigeller.com/

Uri Geller invites you to visit his site and see if you have the potential to become a true psychic force. Check out his interesting life story as well and judge for yourself the results of experiments he has undergone.

Witchcraft

http://www.rci.rutgers.edu/~jup/witches

With Joan's Witch Directory you can explore witchcraft throughout the ages. Based around the 15th century witch hunting manual, the 'Malleus Malificarum', historically correct information and artwork can be viewed.

Reference

Acronyms

http://www.ucc.ie/info/net/acronyms/acro.html

Make sure that your all important name doesn't already exist in business by searching this site's 12,000+ incarnations of abbreviations.

Alt.Culture

http://www.altculture.com/

This popular resource contains a comprehensive searchable a to z of 90's popular culture. Get the news on films, art and music.

Calculators

http://www.calculator.com/

Calculate everything. By using over six thousand tools you can work out the time you will spend sleeping throughout your life to how much food you need depending on your weight in this constantly-updated resource.

Dictionary.com

http://www.dictionary.com/
A site providing the ability to find the language related information you require. Links to huge online dictionaries are here, including the Oxford English.

Encyclopedia.com *

http://www.encyclopedia.com/
Brief articles but fast searches are the name of the game here, at a site containing a massive free Encyclopaedia.

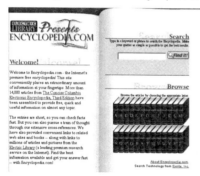

Encyclopaedia Britannica *

http://www.eb.com
The Encyclopaedia Britannica Online. Although only available as a free trial for a seven day period, the idea of an online, constantly updated reference set is virtually irresistible!

English/Cockney Rhyming Slang Dictionary

http://www.bio.nrc.ca/cockney/
Cockney rhyming slang is great, and if you can master it you can baffle and amuse your friends simultaneously. Be warned though. There is no standing on ceremony at this site.

Free Online Dictionary of Computing

http://wombat.doc.ic.ac.uk/foldoc/index.html
If you look at a word like 'bitmap' and have no idea what it means, get online and surf the Web for an answer!

Glossary Of Poetic Terms

http://shoga.wwa.com/~rgs/glossary.html
A back to basics approach for this informative site. Very useful for checking pronunciation before you get to class and embarrass yourself.

Information Please

http://www.infoplease.com
The powerful search engine located at

the Information Please site will find almost anything that you want found. Sport, arts, history, politics – nothing major is neglected.

Multi Media Mapping *
http://uk.multimap.com/
Great detailed maps on any place within England, Scotland and Wales, using a point and click format. Type in a postcode or area name and this will take you straight there. Metaphorically speaking of course.

National Lottery *
http://www.lottery.co.uk

Camelots national lottery site allows you to view previous results, examine number frequencies, and, just for fun, generate six random numbers.

Quoteland
http://www.quoteland.com/
An excellent site for you to find a quote to suit your needs, whether for an essay or just to prove someone wrong. The search facility will also find quotations relating to specific subject matter.

Royal Mail
http://www.royalmail.co.uk
The Royal Mail Website is very useful, since it contains a postage calculator - you input the item that you want to send, and it'll give you the price - to anywhere in the world and using any rate!

Symbols
http://www.symbols.com/
No, not the artist formerly known as Prince, but an incredibly useful online resource with the correct meanings for countless historical, chemical and otherwise bizarre signs.

The Word Police
http://www.theatlantic.com/unbound/wordpolice
Test your English skills to the max, with the Word Police exam! Are you good enough for the force?

Religion

• •

Bible Gateway *

http://www.calvin.edu/cgi-bin/bible/

This comprehensive bible resource is searchable by passage or text reference, which also allows direct linking to its database via the use of hyperlinks.

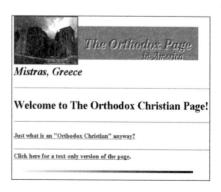

CIN

http://www.cin.org/

Everything related to Roman Catholicism can be found here, from history and papal teachings, right through to recent encyclicals and visits.

Ethical Issues

http://ethics.acusd.edu

A great site for both teachers and students. Many current ethical debates are discussed here, with a relatively unbiased approach.

Global Hinduism

http://www.hindunet.org/

The Global Hindu Network. Teachings, history, culture, philosophy and more are available in this popular religious site.

Insight

http://world.std.com/~metta/

This site focuses mainly on helping practising Buddhists in their meditation technique, understanding teachings and their applications.

Jewishnet

http://www.jewishnet.org.uk/

Jewishnet is the website of Europe's largest online Jewish community. The site provides news, services, shopping and even an online agony Aunt.

Maven

http://www.maven.co.il/

An excellent site with a capable search engine for Jewish or Israeli related links.

Orthodox Christianity *

http://www.ocf.org/OrthodoxPage/

Very well maintained for followers of the

orthodox tradition, or simply those who wish to find out about the faith.

The Vatican
http://www.vatican.va
Stroll around the Vatican's museums, examine the religious statues and artwork and visit the Vatican's own press office.

Science

Annals of Improbable Research
http://www.improb.com/
Most scientists exist to improve and further human existence. Some just explode stuff and do weird things. Some of the latter are here.

Encyclopedia of Psychology
http://www.psychology.org/
Students of psychology will find this an invaluable site when looking for definitions of specialised terms.

European Space Agency
http://www.esrin.esa.it
Basically the less wealthy European version of NASA, the ESA, despite its problems, has had some hands on experience with some very successful space related missions. Have a look at their history and discover their plans for the future.

Frank Potter's Science Gems
http://www-sci.lib.uci.edu/SEP/SEP.html
An entertaining site for either the student or the browser. Physical sciences are the focus here.

Horizon
http://www.bbc.co.uk/horizon
Designed to function as a partner to the excellent TV science series, there are items here from past programmes that tread a truly eclectic path.

IEE
http://www.iee.org.uk/
The Institute of Electrical Engineers site offers information on joining the society, along with a calendar of events, a searchable information database and impressive links to other sites.

The International Space Station
http://station.nasa.gov
Although not quite the same as the space station in 2001, the International Space Station is a reality. A very exciting prospect for anyone wishing to spend long days in the big black.

The Lab *
http://www.abc.net.au/science/
A fascinating site dedicated to the study of all the sciences, with question and answer forums, detailed articles and a wealth of information and links.

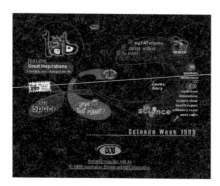

NASA

http://www.nasa.gov

An extremely busy site this one, especially if something big is underway. A great site with information on everything from the Hubble to the Space Shuttle.

The National Museum of Science and Industry*

http://www.nmsi.ac.uk

A well crafted Website with some beautiful collections and fine text. Oh, and a rotating polygon.

New Scientist

http://www.newscientist.co.uk

The Website of the magazine, which has an immense range of interesting articles on a variety of subjects such as earthquakes and cloning.

Nostradamus Society of America

http://www.nostradamususa.com

Some of what is predicted is right, some is wrong. Still, it's not the end of the world.

Nuclear Power Station

http://www.ida.liu.se/~her/npp/ demo.html

Why not try your hand at peaceful nuclear fusion with this interactive nuclear powerplant.

Popular Science

http://www.popsci.com/

Good quality information delivered in an accessible way from the Website of the American magazine.

Rockets Online

http://www.rocketryonline.com/

Almost tongue-in-cheek site giving details on building rockets for science or pleasure, from back garden specials right up to fully-fledged missiles.

Science A Go Go *

http://www.scienceagogo.com/

A very simple and well designed site providing all sorts of news and information from the world of science in a very user friendly manner.

Science Daily

http://www.sciencedaily.com

A constantly updated site with news of scientists who are advancing in their work.

Tomorrow's World

http://www.bbc.co.uk/tw/

In addition to covering the articles on the TV programme this site allows you to delve into the features of past shows.

The X-Prize

http://www.xprize.org

Essentially a competition with a 10 million dollar award, the X-Prize goes out to the first person or group of people to create a working space craft that can be used time and time again, with a long term goal of providing tourist trips to space.

Science Fiction

Alberta UFO Study Group

http://www.planet.eon.net/~kijek

The Alberta UFO Study Group have set up this official page designed to investigate and corroborate stories of UFO sightings in Canada, where some 3 million have occurred.

Aliens are Abducting our Pants

http://www.sock-monkey.com/pants.html

There are a lot of things the people of this world are blissfully unaware of. The fact that aliens are stealing our pants from under our very bottoms is one of them. Lock up your pants!

The Black-Ops Encyclopaedia

http://www.cruzio.com/~blackops

A must for all you conspiracy theorists out there. Although this is essentially still being put together there are some very interesting theories here relating to the Royal Family, Zionism, Presidents and much more.

E.T

http://ebe.allwebco.com

The Extraterrestrial Biological Entity Page. An absolute wealth of information for believers in UFOs and sceptics alike. Containing documented sightings, news reports, chat groups, links and an E.T. search engine.

ExoScience UFO

http://www.exosci.com

Not just specifically UFO related stories, this site has news from NASA and science pages.

Paraweb

http://theparaweb.com

Although there are masses of similar sites around, this online one is a cut above the standard.

X-Files *

http://www.thex-files.com/
The official homepage of the smash
television series. Biographies of
characters, episode rundowns, a fans
forum and links are all included for fans
of the show. Possibly a paranormal
phenomenon itself! But remember, it's
only swamp gas.

Search
Engines

About.com

http://www.about.com
Interested in anything? Anything at all?
You'll probably find it on About.com.
They have a myriad of independently,
professionally updated sites on a whole
range of massively diverse subjects, from
the royal family, to ancient history,

religion and diseases. Each brilliant site
is maintained by an expert on the
subject, and there's no doubt that you'll
find something of interest here!

AltaVista

http://www.altavista.com/
One of the most powerful search engines
on the Internet, you can search web
pages and newsgroups using a single
word, and also include multiple language
searches.

Ask Jeeves

http://www.ask.co.uk
A great place to start if you don't know
where to start! This intuitive engine may
seem basic at first but the unusual use of
actual questions to probe the Internet
can often resault in satisfying
information.

Excite *

http://www.excite.com/
This heavyweight of the search engine
world offers not only a straightforward

search using text entries but also the opportunity to examine its many 'channels where similar sites are grouped together.

Infoseek

http://www.infoseek.com/
Similar to Excite, this search facility offers excellent world wide web search facilities, as well as channels and a customisable format option.

Lycos

http://www.lycos.com/
Lycos provides a great service when you are looking for a very specific topic, with its title-only or URL-only search facilities.

MissInformation

http://missinformation.com
If you're a woman with a question relating to the Internet, ask Miss Information - she's a damned know-all!

Scoot

www.scoot.co.uk
A local directory giving details of hundreds of businesses in any part of the UK. Very easy to use.

Yahoo! *

http://www.yahoo.co.uk
When you have time to really trawl the net, Yahoo! is the engine to use. Its fully featured comprehensive directory

searches are second to none. One for your bookmarks.

Shopping

Alphabet Street

http://www.alphabetstreet.infront.co.uk
Another in the growing line of online stores selling books, music, games and DVD.

Amazon Bookstores

http://www.amazon.co.uk
Choose from 1000s of books online. Read reviews and get recommendations. Pay by secure credit card or by phone if you prefer.

Animail *

http://www.animail.co.uk
An online pet shop where you can purchase a large range of pet related merchandise, including limited edition fine art prints.

The Apple Store

http://www.apple.com/ukstore

This Apple Store site allows you to buy your entire Apple Computer related electronica from the comfort of your own home. Self – explanatory.

Archie McPhee

http://www.mcphee.com/

Buy some quirky gifts for people you know. A voodoo doll. A punching nun. Or even a rubber chicken. Guaranteed hilarity will result.

Audiostreet

http://www.audiostreet.com/

For mainstream rock and pop CDs at discounted prices, in a well laid out site, take a trip down Audiostreet.

Black Star

http://www.blackstar.co.uk/

A massive video store enabling you to search for any title online, as well as search by genre.

Boxman

http://www.boxman.co.uk

Online CD shopping specialist featuring everything from country to techno. Very straightforward.

B&Q

http://www.diy.co.uk/

You can do it with the help of B&Q's excellent site. Get help for all kinds of home or garden projects, find your nearest store and browse through hundreds of hardware products. All the fun of a Sunday without leaving the house.

British Magazines Direct

http://www.britishmagazines.com/

Specialist and mainstream magazines get a look in at this site. Navigate yourself easily around, find a magazine you want and it should be with you in 48 hours.

Bunka

http://www.bunka.co.uk

An online retailer dealing solely in Dreamcast hardware and games.

CD Now

http://www.cdnow.com/
Huge American Web site that sells all music related products from CDs to T-shirts. It can be cheaper to buy from here, despite the postage, than from a UK retailer. Massive array of genres and artists included, and good fun just to browse around.

Chart Deals

http://www.chartdeals.co.uk
Covers the best selling DVD, CD, Video and Books and works out the cheapest place to buy them online. Direct links make it very quick and easy to buy your bargains.

Conran

http://www.conran.co.uk/
An extensive collection of shops that share a common goal, customer satisfaction through customer satisfaction. Excellent product, and competitive pricing. Most products are claimed to be hand picked by Terence Conran Himself!

Cyber Pet

http://www.icatmall.com/cyberpet
An online pet shop which uses a search engine to find products rather than directing you to groups of products. This prevents the site from being as instantly accessible as Animail and The Pet Gift Shops sites.

Dixons *

http://www.dixons.com
Website of Britains leading electrical retailer. Find out the goings on within the company, check out what's new and order online.

DVD World

http://www.dvdworld.co.uk/
A large selection of DVD titles as well as latest news, a search engine and the opportunity to receive weekly mailouts..

Exchange and Mart

http://www.exchangeandmart.co.uk
Buy or sell anything on-line with the classified ads magazine that has become something of a British institution.

Flowers Direct

http://www.flowersdirect.co.uk/
If you left for work in a bit of a huff this morning, return to a home of warmth and happiness by sending some flowers to your loved one!

Fortnum and Mason

http://www.fortnumandmason.com/
Have a look around a virtual Fortnum and
Mason store and if you're not leaving the
house for a while, buy a hamper.

Free Classifieds *

http://www.freeclassifieds.co.uk
Submit and review classified ads for a
wide range of products and services. Pick
up anything from a C-Reg Metro with no
MOT, to a blonde, 24-year-old Taurean
with GSOH, likes walking and fine art.

Gameplay

http://www.gameplay.com
One of the UK's most well known and
trusted games mail order companies.
Gameplay offers news, reviews and, of
course, the option to buy the latest video
games.

GB Posters

http://www.gbposters.co.uk
Hide your wallpaper with a huge
selection of posters. That's the idea with
this site. Music, film, and television
personalities are waiting to adorn your
wall.

Giftstore UK

http://www.giftstore.co.uk
A slightly eclectic range of gifts are
available at Giftstore UK. As well as cards
and flowers, there are also toys, games
and equipment for juggling. You will no
longer be stuck for gift ideas.

Goldfish Shopping Guides

*http://www.goldfish.com/html/guide/
mainset.htm*
Goldfish have teamed up with a range of
companies to offer discounts to their
cardholders. Find out more here.

Heffers

http://www.heffers.co.uk/
One of the oldest bookshops around.
Heffers embraces the Internet with an
excellent site enabling you to order
books on an immense range of subjects.

HMV

http://www.hmv.co.uk/
HMV is one of the UK's leading high
street record, video and video game
retailers. Their website gives you up to
date news, information and special offer
details with the option to purchase online.

Innovations

http://www.innovations.co.uk

Accompanying the catalogue of the same name that falls out of the Sunday papers. Some of the ideas included here are scarecrows, garden swing seats and electric potato peelers.

Interflora *

http://www.interflora.com

Order flowers online for the one you love. With online help and advice and pictures of the flowers to send no-one need be without happiness.

Jungle

http://www.jungle.com

A mail order site selling movies, music, games and computers. The site offers special offers on a wide range of products and loyalty points to keep you coming back.

The Kite Shop

http://www.kiteshop.co.uk

Some of these kites are amazing to look at and very expensive, suggesting that kiting need not necessarily be a child's past time anymore. This site is a must for the serious kite enthusiast.

Let's Buy it

http://www.letsbuyit.com

The idea behind LetsBuyIt is that the more people that buy an item, the cheaper LBI can sell it to you. Could be good as it becomes more popular.

Loot

http://www.loot.com

The online service for second-hand bargains. Place ads and view last weeks advertisements for free, or pay a £1.30 fee to browse the up to the minute bargains.

Macys

http://www.macys.com

Browse around the massive on-line Macys department store. Unfortunately UK customers can't order on-line

My Simon

http://www.mysimon.com

Decide what you want to buy and My Simon will scour the web for the best deals.

NBA Store

http://store.nba.com

Thanks to its highly paid, highly visible stars, Basketball looks set to build upon its reputation as a happening sport over here. This site provides you with the gear you need to look like and play like a pro.

Nutra Source

http://www.nutrasource.com
The place to come if your feeling run-down, want to stay feeling tip-top, or just can't stand the taste of fruit. Buy vitamins, cod liver capsules or even Brain Boost in huge bulk and get huge discounts from this American company.

Off The Record

http://www.otrvinyl.com
An online music shop which specialises in rare and collectible vinyl records. Items can be searched either by a keyword or by genre.

Office of Fair Trading

http://www.oft.gov.uk/
The Office of Fair Trading site offers consumer help with all sorts of trading standards issues. Plus a special section containing tips and advice for shopping on the internet.

Overpriced

http://www.overpriced.co.uk
Are you being ripped off? According to this site, you probably are. It lists dozens of companies according to their 'bad' or 'good' status. Worth checking out.

Pet Gift Shop

http://www.petgiftshop.com
An online pet shop that sells a range of products including books, music, games, animal related jewellery and pet accessories.

Petsmart

http://www.petsmart.com
Not only does the Petsmart site sell its range of products but also includes guides for taking care of your pets and the opportunity to adopt an animal.

Plastercast Skulls

http://www.twoguysfossils.com/ reprod3.htm
Buy reproductions of fossils and even human skulls. The perfect gift shipped to anywhere in the world.

Pricecheck

http://www.pricecheck.co.uk
Cross-reference prices for utilities, cars, mortgages, personal investment and more with this useful online database.

QXL
http://www.qxl.com
Online auction room where you can bid for anything including art, cars, holidays, CDs, games, videos and books.

Richer Sounds *
http://www.richersounds.com/
The online store of the highly regarded bargain hi-fi dealer.

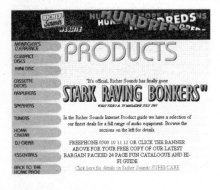

Sainsburys
http://www.sainsburys.co.uk
Shop from home. Check your Rewards balance, get recipes and even play a game of Sergios Crazy Kitchen.

ShopGuide
http://www.shopguide.co.uk
Essential stop for people who want to purchase goods online. This organisation reviews and rates online shopping sites in the UK.

Shopmate
http://www.shopmate.co.uk

Providing links to all the major Internet shopping sites. Decide what type of product you are interested in and Shopmate will supply a brief review of the best online shops available.

Shopper's Universe
http://shoppersuniverse.com
Possibly the best and most complete shopping experience on the Web. Thousands of DIY, games, and sport equipment products are available through this site. Extensive and easy to use.

Shopping Zone
http://shopping.lineone.net
A huge virtual shopping arcade incorporating a huge selection of virtual shops. Everything from music shops through to lingerie shops are featured and rated here, as well as a guide to how secure the online buying is.

Shops On The Net
http://www.sotn.co.uk
Search for a shop on the Web by shop name, topic, address or Website. The site includes details of special offers and lets you know of any new shops starting up, as well as giving its views on current ones.

ShopGuide
http://www.shopsmart.com
Take all the hard labour out of shopping. ShopGuide provides links taking you

directly to the type of shop you need. Plus an excellent bargain finder facility which trawls the net to find you the best deal on whatever you are looking for.

Simply Games

http://www.simplygames.com
A very well presented mail order site providing news and reviews as well as the latest console and PC games at very low prices.

Streets Online

http://www.infront.co.uk
One of the best online shops in the UK. They sell books, DVDs, music and games, at brilliant prices (their top selling books are all half price, with free postage).

Tesco

http://www.tesco.co.uk
The website of the UK's largest supermarket. Contains much more than bread and cheese. Book tickets and holidays on-line, check how many clubcard points you've earned and get free internet access. People living in certain areas can go virtual shopping then have their groceries delivered to their door.

Ticketmaster UK

http://www.ticketmaster.co.uk
Take a trip to the Ticketmaster site to reserve tickets for most upcoming shows or concerts.

Toys R Us *

http://www.toysrus.co.uk
Read the online catalogue, check out the latest promotions and offers and buy toys online.

Unbeatable

http://www.unbeatable.co.uk
A brilliantly designed site allowing you to buy all that is electronic via the Web. Fantastic offers on brand name items are standard with this site, as are the exceptionally detailed specifications.

Sport

All England Lawn Tennis and Croquet Club

http://www.wimbledon.com
Best visited when the championships are in session but still interesting to find out about the history of the place, plus past results and ticket availability and prices.

Autosport

http://www.autosport.com/nav/index.cfm
The website from the bible of the motor racing world. The site provides all the latest news from all aspects of motorsport including Formula One, Rallying and Indycar.

Boxing.com

http://www.boxing.com
When a fight is on, live coverage is available. This is a must for the boxing fan to visit, purely because of the depth of information it provides.

British Touring Car Championship

http://www.btcc.co.uk
Find out where the next meet is, who will be competing, as well as additional information on the teams and drivers.

Bushido Online

http://www.bushido.ch
A brilliant site to look at as the world of martial arts is split open here for all to see.

CarlingNet *

http://www.carlingnet.com
Visit the CarlingNet site for team updates, results, league information and stats.

CricInfo *

http://www.cricket.org
Cricket info covers everything concerning this most British of pastimes. Results, match analysis and news from home and abroad make up this well featured site.

ay 1999

er world record-holding England wicketkeeper, dies aged 78. [Report | Profile]
or defamation by Barbados Police Commissioner. [Report]
omposition of their new nine-man Code of Conduct Commission. [ICC Media Release
s Leicestershire lead the County Championship ladder after the latest round of matches

Lancashire opening batsman Cyril Washbrook dies, aged 84. [Report | Profile]

Cricket Unlimited

http://www.cricketunlimited.co.uk
Concentrating largely on the news aspect this cricket devoted site is kept well up-to-date and details other sites that should be of interest.

Formula1.com

http://www.formula1.com
Not the official Formula 1 site, but a good effort anyway. Terrific photos to look at and very well written stories on the current season.

Golf.com
http://www.golf.com/
A lavish site devoted to all things golfing. The world-wide news is very comprehensive with all the major pro tours are covered, along with rules, equipment and tips to improve your game.

Grand Prix Legends
http://www.grandprixlegends.com
Here you can order Formula 1 merchandise, which apparently is a bit of a blooming industry at the moment. Model cars, helmets, prints, videos and other official goods are available at this site .

Racing Post Online
http://www.racingpost.co.uk
Get the latest racing news, view the runners and riders and see which horses the tipsters fancy.

Rugby *
http://www.scrum.com
Concerned with every aspect of rugby. Find global match results, celebrity viewpoints, find out about women's rugby and even visit the bar!

Rugby Football Union
http://www.rfu.com
An official site packed full of information on the history of rugby, rules, upcoming fixtures and results.

Rugby League
http://www.rleague.com
All the latest info is available here, from match statistics to discussion groups, this is believably self titled as the "most comprehensive Rugby League site".

Sporting Life *
http://www.sporting-life.com
Great resource for fans of all sorts of sports- cricket, racing, snooker, golf, F1, rugby and football are just a few of the national pastimes covered with good depth and accuracy. You can even bet or take part in an online sports quiz!

Wheelbase

http://www.lboro.ac.uk/research/paad/wheelpower/home.htm

The site of the British Wheelchair Sports Foundation providing details of events and competitions. The site also gives contact numbers and addresses for any wheelchair user wishing to take up one of the many featured sports.

Strange

Addicted to stuff

http://www.addicted2stuff.com

A site that asks people to share what it is they are obsessed with. This could be anything from a hatred of poodles to people who mispronounce the word cat. A very funny site, well worth a visit.

The only tools one needs in life:

WD-40 to make things go and duct tape to make them stop.

cars sports pick-up lines bad classified ads good words bad words quotations worrying foodfoodfood ninning things venting & ranting	Hello, Stuff faithful! Welcome to the next evolution of Addicted to Stuff. We have changed a little since the last time you saw us. We have a couple of new categories and a few that we archived. Check out our new Addicted to Sports, Pick-up Lines and Bad Classified Ads!
	Cars From Bronco's to Love Bugs, we love them when they start up, we curse them when

Aliens Ate My Balls

http://artemis.centrum.is/~loftur/ufo.html

A considerably odd site containing a short comic strip about ball eating aliens.

Ask Satan

http://members.aol.com/asksatan/index2.html

A very funny and original site which shows the attempts made by Satan to get some publicity. Great music and hilarious photos of the Devil rubbing shoulders with celebrities.

Casper The Talking Cat

http://www.ibmpcug.co.uk/~artapart/casper

From the Institute of Feline Linguistics comes Casper the talking cat. Although not a huge conversationalist, what utterances he does make are suitably earth shattering.

Conspire *

http://www.conspire.com

Is OJ Simpson part of the Japanese mafia? Is Bill Clinton a serial killer? Are people having brain implants as a part of secret government experiments? Probably not!

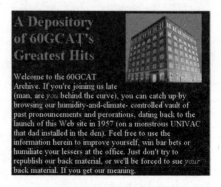

A Depository of 60GCAT's Greatest Hits

Welcome to the 60GCAT Archive. If you're joining us late (man, are *you* behind the curve), you can catch up by browsing our humidity-and-climate- controlled vault of past pronouncements and perorations, dating back to the launch of this Web site in 1957 (on a monstrous UNIVAC that dad installed in the den). Feel free to use the information herein to improve yourself, win bar bets or humiliate your lessers at the office. Just don't try to republish our back material, or we'll be forced to sue *your* back material. If you get our meaning.

Fortean Times

http://www.forteantimes.com/

The Website of the magazine dealing in strange paranoia. The site contains breaking news stories, an archive of articles and much more spooky stuff besides.

ET Corn Gods

http://www.etcorngods.com

Discover hidden subtext within the English language with this site from the ET Corn Gods. Learn how to use their language to bring forth strange stuff.

Guide to Ultimate Reality

http://www.rishi.dk/guide/

Why do things exist? If this is a question to which you have long searched for an answer, have a look here and see if everything suddenly becomes clearer.

Human Radiation Experiments

http://tis-nt.eh.doe.gov/ohre

Provides information on what the title suggests, most of which occurred during the cold war.

I am an idiot!

http://www.iamanidiot.com

A shrine to idiots everywhere - from the woman who wondered what the foot pedal that came with her PC was for (it was the mouse) - to a man who called his ISP's technical support line to try and find help with his lawnmower.

Naked Dancing Llama *

http://www.frolic.org

Take philosophical advice from a Naked Dancing Llama whilst watching him shake his funky thang!

PhoneBashing

http://www.phonebashing.com

The homepage of a bunch of lunatics with an aversion to mobile phones. They run around, stamping on people's phones. There are always moments where you can understand this as perfectly sensible behaviour.

Random Access Memory

http://www.randomaccessmemory.org

Random Access Memory is a database of memories. People can input their own memories of past events - they can be funny, sad, educational or thoughtful. Upon visiting you're presented with a random memory, but you can search for certain themes or names, or add your own memories to the site.

Robot Frank

http://members.aol.com/Broken225/Frank
life.html

Frank the robot is an angry kind of a guy. He's very much like Bender from Futurama - a cynical, scheming type. This site details his life, from gardening and karaoke to ordering in Taco Bell and beating up members of the public.

The T.W.I.N.K.I.E.S Radiation Test

http://www.twinkiesproject.com/
radiation.html

There are a lot of sites devoted to the art of blowing up food. This one is no different as it attempts to blow up a twinkie in a microwave. Science has come a long way.

Viking Remote Viewing

http://www.viking-z.org/

Viking remote viewing, psychic self defence, UFOs and crop circles. Read at your own risk.

Voluntary Human Extinction Movement

http://www.vhemt.org/

A site that tackles the problems connected with the over population of the world by us humans. Sensible solutions are offered in an entertaining way.

Way too Personal!

http://www.waytoopersonal.com

Ever wondered about the stranger people that reply to personal ads? Check out this humourous site to see the downright freaky responses one woman received after putting her ad online. It's hilarious, and well put together - but be warned, it's not suitable for younger readers.

Yashmoo!

http://www.sarrchasm.com/yashmoo

Yahoo is a prime target for mickey taking - and this is the one of the best parodies of it we've seen! It's ridiculous - but it will raise a smile!

Technology

B&W

http://www.bwspeakers.com

At prices ranging from £100 to £35,000, B&W have speakers for everybody and every price bracket, whether you're a paperboy or Richard Branson. Plus a good glossary of terms.

Binatone

http://www.binatone.com/

Sometimes remembered for a somewhat 'budget' feel, the Swiss company's website is anything but that. It boasts music and an excellent online catalogue, which speaks volumes for their sales and marketing departments.

Braun

http://www.braun.de/

Good site dedicated to the German manufacturer of electric toothbrushes and coffee perculators. A very well presented site with good product information proving you can have brains as well as Braun.

Denon

http://www.denon.co.jp

The best of all the Oriental hi-fi makers, Denon have put together this site which allows you to have a look at their equipment, including their new style retro machines, plus lists of stockists.

Hi-Fi Reviews

http://www.whathifi.com

The place to go for up to date news on the ever changing world of Hi-Fi.

Hotpoint *

http://www.hotpoint.co.uk

Very cute animated site with full product line specifications, history, hints and tips

and a spares help section. The company also invite you to contact them regarding a wide range of corporate feedback schemes.

PLEASE NOTE : All information on this web site is relevant only to the UK

We are always keen to hear from you with any views and suggestions as to how we can make the site more informative and useful. Please e-mail

Kenwood

http://www.kenwood-electronics.co.uk/

Take studio quality hi-fi and put it in your car! That's the main point behind this excellent site from Kenwood. There's a section here where you can tailor the best system for your needs.

Linn

http://www.linn.co.uk

For the absolute finest in hi fidelity, check out the Web site from this British manufacturer, Linn. Browse around the vast selections of equipment on offer and then decide if you can afford one.

Philips

http://www.philips.com/

Expansive site from the European consumer giant. Addresses both corporate and home users with a new technologies section that is well worth a look.

Television and Radio

Adbusters

http://www.adbusters.org/

This is a great site for anyone who has ever felt conned and lied to by either a TV or Magazine advertisement. It is a nicely put together swipe at the products themselves as well as the people trying to sell them.

The Adam and Joe Show

http://www.channel4.com/entertainment/ adam_and_joe2/

Adam and Joe's off-the wall humour is broadcast on Channel 4. These teddy bear loving surrealist pranksters will be looking to expand their already large fanbase.

Babylon 5 - Docking Procedures

http://www.babylon5.com

This site can be used by fans who want to discuss and share their opinions on what's great and what grates about this sci-fi series. The usual cast information and clips are available too.

Baywatch *

http://www.baywatchtv.com

If you want behind the scenes gossip on past and present stars of this shiny, happy programme, check out this site and be transported into the sun along with loads of pretty women and hunky men.

BBC Online

http://www.bbc.co.uk

Want a career at the Beeb? There's a vacancies section here, along with all the things the BBC is famous for such as news, weather and education.

Beeb

http://www.beeb.com

Where the BBCs other sites take themselves just a little too seriously, this one is a breath of fresh air. There's a Comedy Zone, a section for Top Gear and something called the Score, where you can get the latest information on all that is sporty.

Brookside

http://www.brookie.com

Get up to date with the plot, view the family trees, buy Brookie products, and take a backstage tour at the official Brookside website. Calm down.

Capital FM

http://www.capitalfm.com/

Shows what will be broadcast and when, special pages allotted to the DJs, plus news and weather.

Carlton *

http://www.carlton.co.uk/

Not just TV listings at this Carlton site, but also sections dedicated to issues raised in the programmes it transmits.

Channel Four

http://www.channel4.co.uk/

A brilliantly designed site, as you might expect from Channel 4. It has information on all the programmes it currently puts out which is put across in a lively, fun and sometimes slightly off kilter way.

CITV

http://www.citv.co.uk

Fun and games with all your favourite childrens ITV television shows in a nice colourful site.

Classic TV Webring

http://www.webring.org/cgi-bin/webring?ring=ctv&list

Timeless TV shows from the 50s to the present day, from the US and the UK are explored in a whole range of independent Websites.

Comedy Central

http://www.comcentral.com/

There's loads of stuff to download at this site as well as providing the opportunity to buy merchandise connected with its programmes, such as the fantastic South Park dolls!

Discovery *

http://www.discovery.com

This site runs in conjunction with the satellite channel of the same name, and very good it is too. As well as details of programmes, the site has loads of science and nature information. There's even a shop to buy stuff!

Driven

http://www.4car.co.uk

The official companion to the Channel 4 show, Driven. Slick and presentable, with more than enough to keep the motoring expert happy.

Dukes of Hazzard

http://hazzard.simplenet.com

A whole host of links and information about Bo, Luke, Daisy, Rosco and good ol' Boss Hogg.

Futurama

http://www.foxworld.com/futurama

The official site of Matt Groenings latest cartoon sensation. The site provides profiles of the cast, a message board, and all the latest Futurama news.

Hollyoaks

http://www.hollyoaks.com

Another of those TV companion sites. Not a huge amount here, but there is some gossip on the show's stars as well as updates.

Jerry Springer

http://www.universalstudios.com/tv/jerryspringer

Get up to date with goings on in the seediest and most talked about show around. Even suggest new topics for shows ("Honey, I'm sleeping with my PC"?)!

NBC

http://www.cbs.com

Perhaps the main focus for this site is The Late Show with David Letterman. Still going strong and still breaking new ground, Letterman's best utterances are reproduced here for all to marvel at.

Radio 1 *

http://www.bbc.co.uk/radio1

Containing all of the latest music and entertainment news, plus the chance to view schedules and playlists. The site also provides webcams, where you get to see the loveable Chris Moyles and co doing their stuff in glorious Technicolor. Best viewed in widescreen!

Red Dwarf

http://www.reddwarf.co.uk

Receive the latest news on the

adventures of Rimmer, Lister, Kryton, Cat and co. Get the stories behind the crew and plots, see below decks and occasionally cyber chat with members of the cast.

Scooby Doo *
http://www.scoobydoo.com
A really fun site providing games and activities for fans of the loveable canine coward. Highlights include a create your own Scooby snack contest, a colouring corner and the haunted gameroom.

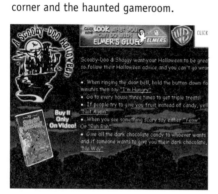

The Simpsons House
http://www.lasvegassun.com/sun/dossier/misc/simpsons/index.html
Ever wanted to dive into your TV and have a nose around the Simpsons Springfield home? Now you can!

Sky
http://www.sky.co.uk
Although providing something of a springboard to all its other channels, this site works best when providing bang up

to date and well-written news and sport.

South Park *
http://www.beef-cake.com
The South Park information centre provides amazingly in depth information on the worlds favourite sick cartoon.

Talkback Productions
http://www.talkback.co.uk
One of the best production companies around at the moment, this site gives an early glimpse of any current projects as well as information about the company in general.

The History of Television
http://www.ebu.ch/dvb_articles/dvb_tv-history.htm
A surprisingly readable and fascinating guide to the history of something we all take for granted. Includes basic diagrams and interesting facts and figures. Surprisingly cool.

They Think It's All Over

http://www.talkback.co.uk/theythink/ index.html

An official site for the often hilarious TV show. Bags of features and competitions await your visit.

Toaster

http://www.toaster.co.uk

A fairly basic but nonetheless useful site containing the entire TV and satellite channel programme listings available in this country.

Trouble

http://www.trouble.co.uk

If you're a regular watcher of this satellite kids channel then you couldn't ask for more. All the programmes are covered, plus games and competitions to have a try at.

Who Wants to be a Millionaire

http://www.phone-a-friend.com

Take a look behind the scenes of the UK's most popular quiz show. View the latest questions, check out the latest news and see pictures and interviews with the past winners.

Theatre and Performing Arts

AWOL

http://www.execpc.com/~blankda/ acting1.html

The Acting Workshop Online. Fascinating site for up and coming actors. Includes invaluable hints tips and advice ranging from basic stage roles to protecting yourself as an artist and making a living. Also contains an online bookshop.

British Actors Register

http://internet-ireland.ie/power/actor

Online showcase for British actors, aimed at agents/casting directors looking for British talent. Gender and alphabetical searches and links to other film and theatre resources. Artists registered include Rik Mayall and Brian Blessed.

Emmys

http://www.emmys.org

The Academy of Television Arts and Sciences. Everything you'll ever need to know about membership, members, and of course the prestigious awards themselves.

RADA

http://www.rada.org

The Royal Academy of Dramatic Art. Details of courses offered, history of the organisation, student showcases and links to other sites including the Conference of Drama Schools.

The Royal Shakespeare Company

http://www.rsc.org.uk
This official site updates you with upcoming productions, news, a box office where you can purchase tickets, and information about past and present performances.

Shakespeare *

http://www.shakespeare.org.uk
The Shakespeare Birthplace Trust. Voted BBC radio 4's "personality of the millennium", Shakespeare's 'homepage' offers historical information, details of museums and houses, a library and an excellent diary of events.

The Shakespeare Birthplace Trust

The Stage

http://www.thestage.co.uk
The UK's only trade paper for theatre and television. Updated weekly, you can advertise your services online as well as view new production details and programme listings.

What's On Stage

http://www.whatsonstage.com
Purchase tickets to the theatre, have a look at the latest theatre happenings around the country and take part in competitions.

Buddy - The Buddy Holly Story

http://www.mpcgroup.co.uk/buddy

Cats

http://www.reallyuseful.com/Cats/index.html

Doctor Dolittle

http://www.doctordolittle.co.uk

Evita

http://www.thenewevita.com

Les Miserables

http://www.lesmis.com

Lord of the Dance

http://www.lordofthedance.com

Mamma-Mia

http://www.mamma-mia.com/

Miss Saigon

http://www.miss-saigon.com/

Phantom Of the Opera
http://www.thephantomoftheopera.com

Saturday Night Fever
http://www.nightfever.co.uk

Transport

The AA *
http://www.theaa.co.uk/
This well presented site offers help and advice, registration details, facts about lead substitute petrol, European cover and basically everything to do with safe driving. Plus a comprehensive hotel search and booking facility.

Auto Trader
http://www.autotrader.co.uk/
Britains biggest source of used cars online. Search for registration numbers, cars and dealers, and advertise your own motor online. Includes a facility to search by make, model, price, age, and even how far you want to travel.

British School of Motoring
http://www.bsm.co.uk/
Information about learning to drive including a section about passing the theory test, with sample questions.

Carsource
http://carsource.co.uk/
Helpful page giving information on new and used cars in the UK. Offers buyers guides, finance help and an excellent search/request facility that links nationwide car dealers.

Hertz
http://www.hertz.co.uk/
Including an online booking service for cars all over the world. Also sections on heavy equipment rental and management information services.

Max Power
http://www.maxpower.co.uk/
The online version of the ultimate boy racers magazine. For enthusiasts of boomin' and cruisin'.

Official Mini Site
http://www.mini.co.uk
40 years of the Mini are celebrated with the full history. There is also a section for designing your own mini online, and some games.

RAC

http://www.rac.co.uk
Well designed site for the Royal
Automobile Club. Features joining
information, live updates on traffic
problems, advice, and special offers.

Railtrack

http://www.railtrack.co.uk/
Providing online timetables and up to
date train information for the UK.

Topcar.com

http://www.topcar.com/
An online magazine containing all that's
new from the world of UK motoring.

Top Gear *

http://www.topgear.com
Online version of the Top Gear TV and
magazine. Car reviews and features all in
that inimitable Top Gear style.

Travel

....

1Ski

http://www.1ski.com/
Lots of skiing information in an easy to
use format, which provides up to the
minute details on any bargains as well as
the all important snow reports.

A2Btravel

http://www.a2btravel.com/
Flights, ferries, insurance, in fact
everything that you need travel-wise can
be found here. Use online mapping, find
out the lowdown on flight departure
delays or even book last minute bargains
with "the UK's biggest online travel
information and booking resource".

ATH

*http://www.cs.cmu.edu/afs/cs/user/
mkant/Public/Travel/airfare.html*
A complete online resource for
everything you will ever need for travel.
Flights, newsgroups, car hire, weather,
tourist information, health, languages,
currency, insurance, maps- the list goes
on. Essential viewing.

Are We Nearly There Yet?

http://www.indo.com/distance/
Calculate the distance between any two
cities, as the crow flies, with this nifty
longitude and latitude library. Great if
you have a helicopter!

Art of Travel

http://www.artoftravel.com/
A backpackers guide to seeing the world
on $25 a day or less. Written by an
experienced trekker this complete online
guide has tips, commentary and humour
for travellers of every kind.

B.A *

http:/www.british-airways.com/
Book online, view special offers, get
traveller's advice and find out about
world-wide airports at the home of
Concorde.

BAA

http://www.baa.co.uk/
Flying away to warmer climates in the
near future? Among many other facilities,
this site allows the traveller to pre order
their duty free selection and collect when
they arrive at the airport. It also details
the most hassle free way of reaching
BAA's UK airports.

Bargain Holidays *

http://www.bargainholidays.com/
Search an online database consisting of
over 70,000 late availability and
discounted holidays- even carry them
with you if you are lucky enough to own
a palm pilot!

Best of Ireland

http://www.iol.ie/~discover/
If you're curious about holidaying in
Ireland, this massive site is your answer.
As well as accommodation and
restaurants, the site has weather
forecasts, popular tourist attractions and
gig guides that cover the country. Some
lovely graphics are included here too,
which more than make up for the
sometimes dry text.

Britannia

http://www.britannia.com/
If you are travelling anywhere within the
UK, this site provides up to date travel
news and accommodation vacancies in
addition to numerous tourist hot spots.

British Foreign Office

http://www.fco.gov.uk

Homepage of the Foreign and Commonwealth office. This is essential for travellers needing to ensure the security of destinations or apply for visas. Also featuring a handy "do's and don'ts" for travellers and a dangerous country blacklist.

Business Traveller Online

http://www.btonline.com

As the title suggests, this site is designed to help the inexperienced business traveller. The standard information is included here – bars, flights, places to eat and hotels, with one eye always on your business requirements.

Campus Travel

http://www.campustravel.co.uk

A site for all those students who backpack thier way through the summer break. Areas covered by the site include cheap flights, InterRailing, American flight passes and details on travelling to and through the Andes.

Club 18-30

http://www.club18-30.co.uk

A very eye catching site this one, but also a bit on the slow side. Nevertheless there's lively information on resorts, hotels and big time partying in general.

Currency

http://www.oanda.com

Over 150 major currencies are covered here including the Euro. Get the latest prices and exchange rates and find out whether to hang on to that left over holiday money.

Deckchair.Com

http://www.deckchair.com

Book flights in this easy to use no nonsense site. Set up to make booking flights on the internet as easy as possible. Great for checking prices in a hurry.

Discount Holidays and Flights

http://www.atuk.co.uk

Lots of attractive women pictured in this site, but it is actually very good. In depth information for budgeting your holiday plans. Car hiring, flights, hotels and local travel are all featured to help you on your way to a cheaper holiday.

Easyjet

http://www.easyjet.co.uk

Web site for the budget UK airline. Allows you to check times and availability of all Easyjet flights and provides secure on-line booking. Excellent stuff if you can travel out of the airports they cover.

EBookers

http://www.ebookers.com

Yet another site for booking holidays and

suchlike. Contains lots of helpful information, good deals, and very useful services for anyone thinking of taking a trip.

Ecotravel Centre

http://www.ecotour.org
A site for the environmentally friendly among you. Ecotravel Centre is dedicated to recommending holiday destinations and operators that are eco-friendly.

Expedia *

http://www.expedia.co.uk
On-line travel agent provided by Microsoft. Book flights, rooms and package holidays departing from the UK. Plus car rental, travel insurance and Last Minute deals.

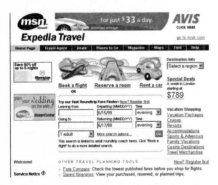

Farebase Electronic

http://www.farebase.net/
This site will practically sort out your entire trip for you. Find a holiday, book a flight and find somewhere to stay by utilising the links it provides. Hire a car and you're sorted.

Go

http://www.go-fly.com
Go is British Airways' economy airline and this attractive looking site provides superb information for those of you wanting to go to Europe and the places to stay in when you arrive.

Infotel

http://www.infotel.co.uk
If you have found a low cost flight from one of the featured sites but still require somewhere to stay, this could be what you are looking for. The site will show what's available near you and will allow you to make a reservation.

Internet Holiday Rentals

http://www.holidayrentals.co.uk/
Photographs and descriptions of homes available for you to holiday in from all over the world. Some of the property is available to buy as well as rent.

Irish Tourist Board

http://www.ireland.travel.ie/
Have a look at some gorgeous scenery courtesy of the Irish Tourist Board. There's information on pubs here too, which is always a must.

ITS

http://www.itsnet.co.uk/
Internet Travel Services offers a comprehensive a to z of all things travel-wise. Travels, pilgrimages and weather

are all covered along with a good last minute flight finder facility.

Last Minute

http://www.lastminute.com

Bargain last minute holidays in both the UK and abroad. Plus special late deals on flights and shows. Last minute deals are also auctioned to the highest bidder. Regular updates on late deals are sent to mailing list subscribers.

Loch Ness

http://www.ipw.com/lochness

Combine a holiday in beautiful Scotland with a little monster hunting. Check out this site if you want to find out how. Lots of pages including information on where to stay, travel and wildlife.

Loco Motives in Ibiza

http://www.housenation.com/loco-motives.htm

Ibiza offers some of the best clubs in the world. If fantastic DJs and fantastic venues are what you're after in a holiday take a trip to this site. Established now for 15 years, Loco Motives provides the best nights out and tells you how to get to and from the clubs, as well as offering discounts and free tickets.

Lonely Planet *

http://www.lonelyplanet.co.uk/

Lonely Planet publishes travel guides on places all over the globe. The site is great companion to the books. Look at photos and get opinions from the people who have been there. Very extensive and simple to use.

National Express

http://www.nationalexpress.co.uk/

Book your long distance coach journey here. Review the fares and the timetables, and find services to major airports.

P&O Cruises

http://www.pocruises.com/

Reasonably good looking site giving you the ability to book your sailing on-line.

Piss up

http://www.piss-up.com

On-line travel agent specialising in cheap boozy citybreaks and heavy drinking festivals. Aimed mainly at students with pick-ups from university campuses throughout the UK.

Pontin's

http://www.pontins.com

A bright and breezy new interactive site ideal for searching for last minute bargains. Use the site to look for Golden Breaks for adults, Family Holidays, Special Interest Breaks and Island Holidays on Jersey and Ireland. Activity programmes are listed in the Family section and Special Offers are exactly that – last minute bargains.

Rough Guide

http://www.roughguides.com

A site that provides all the basic information you might need when choosing a destination and embarking on a holiday. Also provided is a section detailing the views of people who have been to the places included on the site.

Take Off!

http://www.takeoff.beeb.com/

Another impressive site from the BBC with detailed information on the more practical side of holidays. Find a destination from over 226 countries and take heed of the health care information provided.

The Worlds Most Dangerous Places

http://www.abcnews.com/sections/world/dp/dp_intro.html

A site dedicated to the more dangerous places available for your holidays. This is not simply extreme sport but shooting in the streets. Very dangerous stuff. Take the bullet-proof vest not the sunscreen.

Thomson Holidays

http://www.thomson-holidays.com/

You can't actually book a holiday from this site, but it does provide examples of the sort of holidays available through its branches, as well as overseas job information.

Time Out

http://www.timeout.com

Web-site of the ever-popular weekly listings magazine. Contains regularly updated guides to the world's greatest cities, bars, clubs, hotels, restaurants, shops, galleries, museums and music venues. As well as the what's-on listings you will also find features, postcards, maps and classified ads.

Travlang

http://www.travlang.com

The travel and language supersite. Learn the basics for a host of foreign languages, make use of on-line translating dictionaries and book hotels all over the world.

Travelocity

http://www.travelocity.co.uk/
An amazingly comprehensive site, which really does have everything you need, (apart from sunshine), to get you well on your way to the perfect holiday. It even includes a handy currency converter.

UK Street Map

http://www.streetmap.co.uk/
A great way to plan your car journeys across the UK, this site has extensively researched road maps as well as a street map for London.

UK Travel Guide

http://www.uktravel.com
Everything you want to know about travel in the UK. Includes sections devoted to London and The Royal Family as well as a picture gallery, interactive map and on-line store.

Virgin *

http://www.fly.virgin.com/
A packed site home to the worlds 'other' favourite airline. Schedules, booking, travel tips and even a meeting place are all well set out and maintained.

Wish You Were Here?

http://www.wishyouwerehere.com/
A companion site for the ITV holiday show. Like the TV show there are complaints, features on certain destinations and a huge section that covers almost the entire planet.

Weather

B.B.C Weather *

http://www.bbc.co.uk/weather
As with other BBC sites it's service is second to none. 24 hour and five day local forecasts, shipping news and world weather make this site an essential first port of call for your short term weather.

MET Office *

http://www.meto.gov.uk/

Forecasts, news, world links, research and more are all online here at the heart of the UK's favourite pastime.

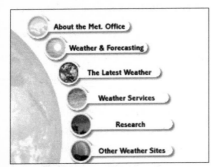

The Weather Channel

http://www.weather.com

Focussed mainly on the weather for America, this Internet version of the cable channel still contains weather forecasts on many regions of the United Kingdom, all displayed in Fahrenheit.

WMO

http://www.wmo.ch

Point your browser towards the World Meteorological Organisation's website for a broader outlook on world weather, storms, climactic changes and weather systems.

World Climate Centre

http://www.worldclimate.com

This site offers long-term weather predictions, in an easy to use city-based search engine. Giving average climate and precipitation figures to get an idea of the general state of affairs weatherwise.

World-Wide-Weather

http://www.intellicast.com

With Intellicast's intuitive system you can view the world's weather with a bulletin posted every half an hour, and a cool radar tracking feature.

Web Broadcasting

Beta Lounge

http://www.betalounge.com

All sorts of gentle dance tracks on offer here. Live performances plus mp3s and a top 5. Won't suit all tastes (we've never heard of these DJs), but it's quite relaxing. Chill out!

Camp Cartoon

http://www.campcartoon.com

Quite the ugliest, crudest Website in the world. However, you can watch Realvideo cartoons from the likes of Porky Pig and Bugs Bunny Daffy Duck and Elmer Fudd. But believe me - it really is very rough so don't get your hopes up.

DiscJockey.com

http://DiscJockey.Com/sixindex.html
A high quality site which provides lots of different channels. You can even make requests online! The adverts tend to annoy slightly, but they are all for large and established companies (such as Yahoo!). Crystal-clear audio and excellent presentation.

Launch

http://www.launch.com
Frankly one of the best sites on the Internet, Launch offers users the ability to compile their own 'stations' of their favourite songs for their own use and for their friends. You can also watch loads of music videos - and all free of charge!

Like Television

http://www.liketelevision.com
If you've ever wanted to watch complete movies or TV episodes over the Internet, this is the best (legal) way of doing so. There are plenty of films here. All of them are reasonably old, most black and white

- but there are some real classics, including Night of the Living Dead and Little Shop of Horrors. All of the films and TV series are organised into categories, such as science fiction and comedy. The frame rates aren't ideal, but it's pretty impressive stuff an free!

Mondo

http://www.ugo.com/animation/Mondo/default.shtm
What, online broadcasting without Realmedia or ASF? Yes, this uses Shockwave to display animations, which means that the quality is absolutely stunning and download times are very, very short. The content is in the form of episodic cartoons. Amusing, and worth the effort.

On The Air

http://www.ontheair.com
A huge list of online radio stations and other streaming audio providers. An absolutely massive site, which lists over 1500 radio and TV stations that broadcast online. It hasn't been updated in six months at the time of writing, but the Web directory is still very useful. Also lists over 400 Webcams.

Real

http://www.real.com
Download RealPlayer - the standard package for streaming video and audio over the Internet. Real also has a good

content guide to get you started.

Sky Radio

http://www.skyradio.nl
Get down to all of the latest pop hits
courtesy of this great European station.
The jingles and songs are in English, but
the rest isn't. If you can put up with that
this is a great site.

Triple J

http://www.abc.net.au/triplej/triplej.htm
The very best in Aussie pop music, from
Rolf Harris to... er... INXS and Kylie. Good
quality audio.

Wild West TV

http://www.wildwesttv.com
In much the same vein as Camp Cartoon
(and by the same people), this site
contains movies and TV shows on a
western theme. Ugly as hell and crude
too - but it works.

Web Cameras

Africam

http://www.africam.com/
See live happenings at watering holes at
some of Africa's game reserves. Updated
every 30 seconds

Almost Amazing Turtle Cam

http://www.campusware.com/turtles/

Receive live pictures of two turtles in a
tank. Updated every 60 seconds

Earthcam

http://www.earthcam.com/
Searchable directory of catagorised
webcams throughout the United
States.

Medano Beach, Cabo San Lucas, México

Fat World Cam *

http://www.fat.co.uk/world/worldset.html
Random pictures from over 100 live web
cams from all over the world.

JennyCam *

http://www.jennicam.org

Possibly the most famous webcam. Follow the life of Jenny, the woman who gets absolutely no privacy.

Kremlin Kam

http://www.kremlinkam.com/
Provides live pictures of the Kremlin

Llama Cam

http://www.lioby.com/cam1.htm
Live llamas taking part in wacky daily adventures......not!

NASA Web Cams

http://www.ambitweb.com/nasacams/nas acams.html
Live pictures from the Kennedy Space Centre, watch the goings on in the main control areas.

Nerdman Show

http://www.nerdman.com/
Bills itself as a real life Truman Show using 17 cameras at home and work to keep you up to date with the adventures of Nerdman.

New York Cab Cam *

http://www.ny-taxi.com/
This one's pretty cool. Ride around in a New York Taxi live anytime between 7am and 7pm US Eastern Time. Your host is New York's number 1 cabby Clever Da Silva who wrote the book New York City from A Cab Driver's View which, surprisingly, is available to buy on the website.

Planet Timmy

http://www.planettimmy.com
Enter the wild world of Timmy a 26 year old computer games programmer from Guildford

Popocatepetl

http://www.ssec.wisc.edu/data/vol cano/popocat.html
Provides live aerial views of the Popocatepetl volcano in Mexico

Sam's Webcam Cookbook

http://www.teleport.com/~samc/bike/
Gives instructions on how to set up your very own webcam

The Student House

http://www.studenthouse.net
Keep an eye on the zany and most probably drunken adventures of four students sharing a house in Sheffield. Don't bother trying before 6pm though. They're all in bed asleep.

Terraserver
http://www.terraserver.com/
A site from Microsoft supplying digital satellite images of Cities across the US and elsewhere.

Worldwide Webcam top 100
http://www.worldwide-top100.com/topsites1
Lots of Webcams listed so that you can spy on members of the public! Some slightly risque sites listed, but nothing too adult.

Web Design

Builder.Com
http://www.builder.com/
A site that goes to great trouble and depth to show how best to go about developing a web site. Hints, tips and a reference library are all provided.

The CGI Resource Index
http://www.cgi-resources.com/
If your interests lie in CGI Programming, check out this site for 'here's one I made earlier scripts' as well as helpful advice for the layman and the expert.

Internet.Com
http://www.internet.com/
News on and about the Internet and the technology that surrounds it. Articles and features abound, rubbing shoulders with loads of reference material.

The Internet Traffic Report
http://www.internettrafficreport.com/
The traffic of data is monitored here as well as the amount of time it takes the world's foremost key routers to respond. If this excites you and you require more information, visit the site.

The W3C
http://www.w3c.org/
This company devotes itself to promoting high standards on Web sites as well as professionalism. Some of the criteria it wishes to be met can be accessed here, as well as some background information on the Internet.

Worst of the Web *
http://www.worstoftheweb.com/
A self-descriptive Web site, which works not just to indicate what not to do, but also shows examples of some hilariously awful sites.

worst (wurst). - adj. 1. Most inferior, as in quality, condition, or effect. 2. Most severe or unfavorable. 3. Furthest from an ideal or standard; least desirable or satisfactory. 4. See www.worstoftheweb.com

Weekends and Days Out

• •

British Tourist Authority
http://www.visitbritain.com
Official site, set up more for those visiting Britain than nationals, but lots of great information for everyone. The site looks great and the accommodation section is very thorough, with ratings and details on a huge number of places to stay.

Northern Ireland Tourist Board
http://www.ni-tourism.com
The official site. Good level of information on travel essentials in a clear and straightforward site. Ideal for planning a visit.

Scottish Tourist Board *
http://www.holiday.scotland.net
Great looking official site. Lots of information including itineraries, accommodation, activities, and travel tips.

Welsh Tourist Board
http://www.visitwales.com
Not a great deal on this site. Links off to other sites to provide information. What it does is fine, but there is not much here.

Knowhere Guide to Britain
http://www.knowhere.co.uk
Great site with insider views of over 500 British towns. Can however be downbeat.

Alderney
http://www.alderney.gov.gg
Lots of photos and a straightforward layout for the Island's tourist information. You can also email for a free brochure.

Guernsey
http://tourism.guernsey.net
All the usual travel information on this official tourist board site.

Jersey
http://www.jtourism.com
Clear site providing accommodation, what to see and do, travelling, and a brochure request form.

Places of Interest
British Waterways
http://www.british-waterways.org/
Official site covering boating, fishing,

and canal holidays.

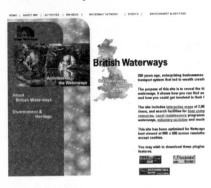

Lake District
*http://www.wwwebguides.com/britain/
cumbria/lakes/lakes.html*
General information on the Lakes and the
towns and villages of the region.

North Wales Tourism
http://www.nwt.co.uk/
Covers places of interest and
accommodation. Information about
Snowdonia is included.

Scottish Highlands
http://www.host.co.uk/
Great looking, slow loading. This official
tourist board site covering
accommodation, activities, events and
even video footage.

Stones of England
*http://utenti.micronet.it/dmeozzi/
England/England.html*
Covers ancient stone circles and the like
with directions of how to get to them.

Cities
Belfast
http://www.tourism.belfastcity.gov.uk
Clear and well laid out site with well
presented information.

Blackpool
http://www.blackpool.gov.uk/btourism.htm
The official site, covering the usual facts,
though not in huge detail. There is a free
brochure request form though.

Bournemouth
http://www.bournemouth.co.uk
Unexciting with big lists of information.
Very text heavy but simplistic. Ideal for
sorting your stag night.

Brighton
http://www.brighton.co.uk
Fine presentation, with restaurant
reviews, accommodation guide and
attractions. Lots of good maps and
information on travelling.

Cardiff

http://www.cardiff.gov.uk.
Official site including accommodation, places of interest and travel information. You do have to hunt around for it though!

Chester

http://www.chestercc.gov.uk/tourism/home.htm
Official government site that covers the standard travel information in a clear way.

Edinburgh

http://www.edinburgh.org
Official site covering the important travel information. Plus useful links to anything that the site does not cover.

Glasgow

http://www.glasgow.uk.com/
Tourist information, accommodation, maps and even a web-cam. Basic site design.

Liverpool

http://www.merseyside.org.uk
Very heavy style to the site, which is interesting but annoying to navigate if you just want the facts.

London

http://www.londontown.com
Official great looking site. Loads really slowly, but it does have excellent presentation. Accommodation, dining, attractions, pubs, maps and shopping.

Manchester

http://www.manchesteronline.co.uk/guide
Part of the Manchester Online site covering the usual tourist essentials.

Newquay

http://www.newquay.org.uk/
Good site covering accommodation, the beaches and surfing. Includes an online brochure request form.

Oxford

http://www.oxfordcity.co.uk/
Very good site covering the city, with a great accommodation section and a smart clear layout.

York

http://www.thisisyork.co.uk/
Published by the Evening Press paper this site covers all tourism issues along with much more.

Theme Parks

Alton Towers

http://www.alton-towers.co.uk

Examine the rides, find out about pricing, see what special events are on, find out how to get there, and get tips to make the most of the park.

American Adventure

http://www.adventureworld.co.uk/

Covers the attractions, special events, and admission prices. Plain, but effective.

Blackpool Pleasure Beach

http://www.bpbltd.com/

Stylish official park site. Details of the park, tickets, events and shows. You may have to click on the non-java menu on the opening screen to view it though!

Drayton Manor

http://www.draytonmanor.co.uk

Clear layout covers prices, location, and general park information.

Great Yarmouth Pleasure Beach

http://www.pleasure-beach.co.uk/ frameset.htm

Unexciting site contains pricing information, photo's and location information.

Lego Land

http://www.legoland.co.uk/

Lego feeling site with all the ride, show, special event and booking information neatly presented. You can even book tickets online.

Longleat

http://www.longleat.co.uk/

Lots of information on pricing and getting to the park. Nothing on the animals though.

Thorpe Park

http://www.thorpepark.co.uk

Simple site that covers the major rides, pricing and location of the park. The site is not the easiest to navigate due to the odd headings such as Mums and Dads.

Glossary

....

ActiveX	Microsoft's answer to Java. Allows programs to run in a Web window.
Attachment	A File sent with an Email.
AOL	America Online. An international content provider.
AVI	Microsoft's famous compressed video format.
Bleem!	PlayStaion emulator.
Bandwidth	The size of a data connection which carries Internet traffic. More bandwidth means more possible traffic at any given time.
BBS	Bulletin Board System. What people used before the Internet hit the mainstream. The poor fools.
Bookmarks	Netscape's way of keeping a list of your favourite Web sites.
Browser	A program used to browse the World Wide Web.
Cache	An amount of disk space used by a Web browser to store recently visited Web sites for quick retrieval.
Cookie	Small text file which sites can store on your computer so that when you return to the site it already knows your information.
Cracker	Somebody who hacks into computers with malicious intent. Also somebody who breaks the copy protection on commercial software for distribution in pirate channels.
DCC	The method of sending files over IRC.
Domain name	An Internet address, such as Altavista.com.
Download	Transfer a file from a machine on the Internet to your own computer.
Email	Electronic Mail.
Emulation	A way of running software on a computer that it was not designed for.
FAQ	Frequently Asked Questions. An explanatory text file put together by somebody who is fed up of answering the same questions over and over again.
Favourites	Internet Explorer's way of keeping a list of your favourite Web sites.
Finger	A program which can be used to gain information concerning particular users of the Internet. Only works if they have an account on a UNIX based operating system (a hint - most people don't!).

Flame	An angry/abusive attack on somebody in a Newsgroup.
FTP	File Transfer Protocol.
GameSpy	A program used to assist anybody playing online games.
Gopher	A system used for downloading files. Now pretty much obsolete.
GUI	(Pronounced 'gooey') Graphical User Interface. A means of using software through the mouse rather than, for example, the keyboard.
Hacker	Somebody who 'breaks in' to computers on the Internet.
Half-life	Extremely popular online game.
Header	The beginning of an Email message which is concerned with the addressing and the identity of the sender.
HTML	Hypertext Markup Language. The language of the World Wide Web. All Web pages are written in HTML.
HTTP	HyperText Transfer Protocol. The protocol for web communications.
ICQ	A very popular piece of software for keeping track of your friends when online, and general chatting.
IP Address	A series of numbers which designate the unique location of each computer on the Internet.
IRC	Internet Relay Chat - One of the most popular ways of talking online.
ISDN	Integrated Services Digital Network. The standard for digital telephone communication. Allows Internet access at 12k per second, if you can afford it.
ISP	Internet Service Provider. Your gateway to the Internet. Most of these are free services, you just pay local call rates to connect to them.
Java	A program language that is designed to produce programs which should, in theory, be able to run on almost any modern operating system.
JPEG	The most-used picture format on the Internet. Allows high amounts of compression. It is a *lossy* format - this means that the better the compression, the worse the image quality.
Kill File	A function which enables the user to block mail from Spammers.
Lamer	Rude term for somebody who is either computer illiterate or simply stupid.
LAN	Local Area Network. An independent network, which may or may not be connected to the Internet.
LINUX	A freeware operating system, based around UNIX. Runs many UNIX programs and can run on any PC above a 386. Famous for being fast and very efficient.
MIDI	Musical Instrument Digital Interface. In the context of online use, MIDI files contain information for synthesizers. Computers can play these files

too, however, and they take up only a minute amount of disk space. Sometimes only a few Kilobytes for five minutes of music. Sound quality is often akin to that of a 1980s electronic organ, unfortunately. MIDI files are often (far too often) used as background music on Web pages.

Mosaic　The first ever Web Browser. Available on PC, Mac, Unix and Amiga. Now totally outdated. Netscape was originally based upon Mosaic.

MP3　The MPEG format for storing sound files. CD Quality sound can be stored at around one Megabyte per minute of audio.

MPEG　One of the most popular forms of compressed video files.

Netiquette　The way one should conduct onself on the internet.

Newbie　Somebody who is new to using the Internet or a particular aspect of it.

Newsgroups　The world's biggest bulletin board system. Works in conjunction with Email.

NNTP　The standard for dealing with Newsgroup postings.

Ping　A program used to check if a host is available, or how fast it is relative to your location.

Plugin　A file used to upgrade or work with another program, such as a Web browser.

POP3　Post Office Protocol. The most often used format for Email servers.

Proxy　A proxy is an invisible server that sits between you and the Internet. It downloads files that you request and then sends them to you. They're usually used to act like a cache - they store previously downloaded Web pages on them that will be sent to you whenever you request that Web site. Sometimes they are used to monitor or control Internet sites visited.

Quake/II/III　Two of the most popular games for online use. See 'GameSpy'.

RealAudio　An Audio format created to allow 'streaming' audio over the Internet - that is, sounds that play as they download. Often used by Radio stations (such as Virgin) to transmit their shows over the Internet. See http://www.real.com

RealVideo　RealAudio's big brother - video and audio both at once.

Search Engine　A huge searchable database of Web sites. They usually use programs called 'Robots' to seek out and list all of the Web sites they can find.

Server　A machine on the Internet used to make information or services available to people.

SMTP　Simple Mail Transfer Protocol. A type of server used by many ISPs to send users email.

Smiley　An emotive symbol used to express humour or sadness when chatting or using Newsgroups. For example, :-) is happy, and :-(is sad. You have to

	imagine them turned 90 degrees clockwise to see how they work.
Spam	Junk Email, named Spam after a Monty Python sketch. Sadly, Spam is not yet illegal. Almost all Spam mails contain information concerning illegal scams, however. Never, ever buy anything advertised via an unsolicited email.
Surfing	The media friendly term for using the internet.
Talker	A program running on a machine (usually Linux or UNIX) which allows people to connect to it and chat to one another.
Telnet	Allows you to log into remote computers. Used for direct computer access and talkers.
Troll	Somebody who delights in causing controversy or getting on people's nerves. Usually refers to Newsgroup posters.
UNIX	A very old and largely text-based Operating System, still used by most serious Internet users (such as large businesses and most or all ISPs).
URL	Uniform Resource Locator. A Web address.
UUEncode	A method of encoding binary files for sending via Email or Newsgroups. Most News/Email clients can automatically encode or decode these files.
Virus	Hidden programs which can corrupt your software.
Vivo	A form of streaming video.
Warez	Pirated software.
Web site	A collection of documents published on the Internet.
WWW	World Wide Web. A huge network of documents, consisting of text, graphics, sound and video. The World Wide Web is not the Internet - just a part of it.
WYSIWYG	What You See Is What You Get. How you see something on screen is the way it will really turn out.
ZIP	The most popular form of compression for files being transferred over the Internet. Get a copy of WinZip from http://www.winzip.com.

Abbreviations & Smileys

AFAIK	-	As Far As I Know
AFK	-	Away From Keyboard
ASAP	-	As Soon As Possible
ATM	-	At The Moment
BBS	-	Be Back Soon
BBL	-	Be Back Later
BF	-	Boyfriend
BRB	-	Be Right Back
BTW	-	By The Way
CU	-	See You
FYI	-	For Your Information
GDI	-	God Damn It
GF	-	Girlfriend
IMHO	-	In My Humble Opinion
IRL	-	In Real Life
LOL	-	Laughs/Laughing Out Loud
PPL	-	People
RL	-	Real Life
ROFL	-	Rolls On the Floor Laughing
ROTFL	-	Rolls On The Floor Laughing
RTFM	-	Read the Flipping (!) Manual
TTFN	-	Ta Ta For Now
WTF	-	What/Who/Where/When The Flip (!)
WWW	-	World Wide Web

Often in chat, emotives have to be expressed in the form of smileys. Emotion can't always be read into normal text, and smileys can prevent people from taking sarcastic comments seriously. Turn the book on it's side to turn the following characters into smiley (or otherwise!) faces.

:-)	-	Smiling
;-)	-	Winking. Used when joking etc.
;-P	-	Tongue out
;-P~	-	Tongue out and dribbling
:-D	-	A big teethy smile!
:-S	-	Oops!
:-/	-	Can mean glum, unsure, sceptical, sighing etc.
:-(	-	Sad
:~(	-	Crying
:-)))	-	Very happy.
:-0	-	Shouting
>:-)	-	Devious

definitive
guide to internet
travel

All the travel information you'll ever need is on the internet

- How can get the best holiday deal?
- Whats the weather going to be like when I get there?
- Is it safe?
- How do I know the brochure is correct?
- Where can I get a free map or guide?

Get the fast and simple answers to these and thousands more questions. The Internet is an unrivaled source of information on all aspects of travel. From Youth Hostels to luxury Hotels, from Bradford to Barbados, business or pleasure, you can find everything you need to know. But finding it can take forever. This guide will show you how to get straight to details you need without fuss or technical jargon.

Containing a comprehensive directory of over 1000 websites dedicated to travel and tourism in virtually every country on the planet to help take the stress out of your trips.

Find thousands of bargain holidays and flights – Discover the best places to visit and stay – Get instant weather and travel forecasts – Receive impartial information – Learn about different languages, customs and cultures – Work your way around the world

Whatever you need for whatever reason, this guide will prove an essential tool.

2000 uk edition

definitive
guide to internet
travel

only
£7.99

publishing

the definitive travel guide using the internet

www.fkbonline.co.uk